On Our Own
Widowhood for Smarties

a Silver Boomer Book

collection compiled by:

Thelma Zirkelbach
Barbara B. Rollins
Becky Haigler
Robyn Conley

www.SilverBoomerBooks.com
~§~
SilverBoomerBooks@gmail.com

Library of Congress Control Number: 2012912104
ISBN: 978-1-937905-16-3

Printed in the United States of America

Table of Contents

"Death ends a life, not a relationship." Mitch Albom ~§~ "It is better *to be the widow of a hero than the wife of a coward." Dolores Ibarruri*

~§~ *"Memory, in widow's weeds, with naked feet stands on a tomb-*

stone." *Aubrey de Vere* ~§~ *"Widow. The word consumes itself." Sylvia*

Plath ~§~ *"The friend who can be silent with us in a moment of de-*

spair or confusion, who can stay with us in an hour of grief and be-

reavement, who can tolerate not knowing...not healing, not curing...

that is a friend who cares." Henri Nouwen ~§~ "Where you used to be,

End and Beginning

Thelma Zirkelbach

October sun streamed across your face
As you took your last breath.
Trapped in a hospital bed, surrounded by rails,
   unable to walk—
You were free at last.
And I was left behind.

When I shuffled toward the exit, the nurses barely
   glanced at me.
The room where you fought your battle needed
   cleaning,
The ground prepared for another
Fight for life.
Patients are interchangeable.

I trudged into the sunlight,
Into the dark,
Along the rocky path of widowhood,
Ringed by ghosts,
Pierced by memories.

there is a hole in the world which I find myself walking around in the

Five years now I've walked alone
Maneuvered twists and turns.
Learned to stand upright.
Sturdier now, muscles forged in fire
And in ice.

Insulated Answers

Maura MacNeil

There was so much to do to prepare for winter, I didn't know where to start. My husband had been a jack-of-all-trades, a resourceful man. He could fix anything, and when it came to winterizing our home, situated on the side of a mountain in the southwestern region of New Hampshire, he was an organized master. I never paid attention to these things; I would arrive home from work one day and the air conditioner would be in the utility closet, the lawnmower drained of gas and stored away, the crawlspace pipes insulated, the furnace softly humming.

I began with the familiar: I made lists. I knew how to do that. I made lots and lots of lists. Brightly colored Post-It Notes littered the house like confetti. I would shut my eyes and conjure the image of Barry readying the property for winter and I would write down what I imagined. Over the course of a few weeks I made some headway – storm windows cleaned and inserted: check; draining and winding up the garden hose: check; placing the roof rake in a place easily accessible after a snowstorm: check. I told myself that focusing on these tasks, learning new skills, was healthy for my grief. It gave me purpose, a feeling I had lacked since the moment I kissed his forehead and whispered goodbye in the emergency room of the regional hospital after a fatal heart attack had taken his life.

But the *bowels*, as I began to call them, of the house were another matter. I had never, ever thought about plumbing or heating. I simply turned a faucet on and off, turned the thermostat higher or lower depending on my need for comfort. Never once had I taken a hard look at the pipes, let alone thought long and hard about how pipes connected to faucets, or how they ran into the house. I knew where the hot water heater was located only because it was in a small closet next to my own clothes closet and I viewed it as something that denied me extra room for my clothes. And wasn't there something I should know about the heating tape on the pipes?

I couldn't stop thinking about that first January in our home when the region was hit with a sub-zero cold snap with high winds that lasted for more than a week. On a Sunday morning, as I lay in bed with the flu, the pipes froze. I was alerted to this by Barry's stomping around the house from faucet to faucet as if his heavy footsteps could shake the house hard enough to make the water run. Armed with my hair dryer, he squeezed into the crawlspace beneath the house and within minutes, it seemed, the water was running again. Moving in and out of sleep with a box of tissues by my side I croaked out, "Have you taken care of it?" He assured me he had. Through the remainder of the week he monitored faucets like the solider he once was; he vowed he would never go under the house armed with hair dryer again.

Twelve years later I was alone and I entertained the idea of apartment or condo living as winter approached. Some mornings, heavy with grief, it was all I could do to get out of bed and move through the workday. How could I add a whole new skill set to my life, one that included taking care of a house that had a personality I hadn't taken the time to get to know? I didn't need purpose. I needed my husband to reassure me. I began to run through emergency scenarios in my head, situations that in the past Barry would have taken care of. I began to obsess about frozen pipes, leaking pipes, bursting pipes. No matter how hard I tried as the scenarios played out in my imagination, I couldn't imagine crawling under the house with my hair dryer in subzero temperatures. Friends began passing me names of their plumbers when I expressed doubt about how I would "figure it out." But those names disappeared from my widow-memory quickly. Business cards were lost. I wasn't ready for someone to take Barry's place, even if it simply meant someone to crawl under the house.

Five months into widowhood I rationally under-stood that Barry would not be coming back. I was alone in a house on twenty-two acres in an isolated rural community with an elderly demanding dog and a house infrastructure as foreign to me as Chinese Mandarin. I had to figure out a way to make it work, but my growing lists woke me up in the middle of the night. My lists were what I thought about when I woke up to morning's first light, what I added to when I drank my morning coffee. My to-do lists were colliding in the twisted crossroads between wanting to prove to myself I could survive on my own, and the desire to do it the way "Barry did it" so that everything, for just a little bit longer, would feel the same as it had been when he was alive. I refused help despite a desperate need for it. I believed the spirit of my husband would guide me.

In the first week of October I squeezed into the crawlspace to study the pipes. I met with a twisted chaos of pink fiberglass insulation wrapped and stuffed around *something*. Mouse droppings littered the concrete slab and I breathed heavily behind a cotton facemask, my clear plastic protective goggles fogging up with each breath released. This really sucked.

The first step was to peel away the layers of insulation so I could see exactly what I was working with. I needed courage more than sense. There were mice. I hate mice. Give me snakes, spiders, frogs and toads, but don't give me mice. It went back to childhood when I found a nest of newborn mice in the corner of my closet. Pink and hairless, they squirmed like fat worms and I felt sick to my stomach. The image returned and I felt nauseous. And utterly alone.

I closed my eyes and conjured the image of Barry and I spoke to him as I so often did since his death: *Barry, what are these valves for? What do I turn? What do I do?* My pleas were prayer. I pushed my way out of the crawlspace and knelt in the dirt and wept. This was my life now – this tangle of insulation, this highway of pipes I needed to understand in order to understand myself.

The answer I looked for did not concern the mess in front of me. Through my tears I knew that. The real answer I searched for was whether Barry, in death, would continue to keep me safe. He died so suddenly, so unexpectedly, but days after his death I discovered that he had put all of his affairs in order. He knew he was dying, maybe not consciously, maybe he didn't use those words for himself, but he had organized everything so I would not have to piece together a puzzle of legal papers through guesswork. In life he protected me, took care of me. The days following his death were a profound reminder of that. Now that he was gone, couldn't he still somehow continue to do so for as long as I needed?

What gets me through the days are small victories. Changing light bulbs, installing a new lock on the door, washing Barry's truck in the do-it-yourself spray bay of the local car wash. Sometimes getting up in the morning feels like a victory as I make my way down the hallway, lured by the thought of coffee, hopeful that the day ahead will not reveal calamity. I am learning through small victories, but what about those things I have no idea how to learn to do on my own?

Barry took care of everything. How could I understand the intricacies of plumbing when I was doing all I could do to keep myself from shattering apart? That night, after going under the house and feeling defeated and alone and scared, I lay in bed and listened to the house creak and groan against hard wind. The sound might as well have been Barry's voice. It told me loud and clear that I could not do this on my own. I was ready to listen.

The following morning I called a plumber. It is what I should have done all along. His receptionist was willing to listen to my story. "I am a widow. My husband took care of things. I am not sure what it is I need." Through her willingness to listen I found myself trusting someone, through a phone line, and that was another step forward I needed. "My husband knew how to do things that I don't know how to do," I told the plumber when he arrived a week later. He is kind and looked at me that first time with compassion. I also detected a small measure of concern.

That night, the crawlspace insulated well against the harshest winter that could be thrown, I sat in the living room with a glass of wine listening to a wind that signaled winter was close at hand. The dog snored loudly on the floor beside me and it was comforting. I knew that night I might be able to do this thing called living. I might not do it well all the time, and I might have to admit defeat more often than I like, but this living meant not only a strong measure of prayer but a small measure of help. I believe if Barry is looking down on me he would agree.

There's No One

Lessa Roskin

There's no one to tell me
What to do
When to do
How to do
Why to do
With whom to do
Where to do
If to do
Not to do
Should I do
Can I do it NOW?

Widows' Walk

Charlotte Wolf

Recently bereft, we share
summer novels, catch all the latest movies
obsessively attend church, committee meetings
and Great Books discussions, attempt
to nourish our souls.

Sharing impromptu lunches and suppers out
indiscriminately, so there's someone to talk to
we swallow semi-healthy, semi-tasteless food
but don't do dishes

share gifts of laughter, tears and sympathy
and our grief, understanding it will always be there
worship busy-ness as manically, we fill our week-
at-a-glance calendars, scorning empty spaces
the new enemy is time.

Alone, with no sound of familiar in the silent rooms
we watch endless reruns on TV, make frivolous
calls to a friendly voice, hold conversations
with the cat, the mailman, the water-meter lady.

W. S. Merwin ~§~ "When you are sorrowful look again in your heart,

We walk the crippled walk of half a person
along a path not chosen, genuflect
before the refrigerator, the new altar
of magnetized memories: once-upon-a-time family
anxiously check our calendars for the next meeting.

Widowed

Susanne Braham

Being no longer
reveals how much you were.

I stumble on;
two legs are less than four.

Lacking one for balance,
one for joy,
I sample panoplies of crutches.

Some make do.
None supports like you.

I Know She Is Dead

Peter D. Goodwin

Over two years – dead
her absence accepted
life – my life continues
without her – yet
whenever I fail
to turn off the toaster oven
I hear her voice
You'll have us all burnt down
or leave the front door unlocked
We'll be murdered in our sleep
or leave the toilet seat up
or commit so many other small sins
I still hear
her irritated response
and I stare at the ceiling
I smile
pretend I don't hear her
as if she is still here.

What I Learned When My Husband Died

A guide for women who are still married because their husbands didn't die.

Nina Abnee

I heard the ringtone on my iPhone playing Simon and Garfunkel's "Homeward Bound," a signal that "home" was calling. The digital clock on my dashboard said six p.m. Tears slowly ran down my face and dropped onto the steering wheel. I was struck with overwhelming sadness like a hot flash that randomly washes over you. I glanced at my phone on the passenger seat. It wasn't ringing. Unless my dogs had figured out how to use speed dial, there was nobody home to call me.

Victor called me every night around six and every night he asked the same question, "What's your Theta?" It was his way of asking, "When will you be home." He was non-judgmental about the answer.

Whatever I said was fine. *Will be on my way in five minutes. It will be hours. I'm in a meeting. I'll call you later.* And he knew that if I said *soon*, it could mean an hour or more.

He'd respond with something like, "The kids want to watch *Friends* at nine and we are having chicken for dinner."

I'd reply, "I will be home by nine then." And I would be. All very casual. Never an argument. Non-eventful. But he always included a little incentive to get me home. Not the chicken. He only knew how to make three things for dinner and they all involved a can of Campbell's cream of mushroom soup. Rather, something he knew I wouldn't want to miss.

He knew how to gently reset my priorities and tell me to shut it down at work and come home without ever saying, "Shut it down at work and come home."

The thing is, I didn't realize any of this. I learned it the hard way.

We found out he was going to die three weeks before he did. The cancer that was supposed to be treatable wasn't behaving as we expected. Dr. Benson leaned over Victor's bedside on a Monday morning and said with eerie calmness in his voice that the pathology was clear. The diagnosis was correct, neuroendocrine carcinoid. (In other words, we did not make any mistakes.) The tests indicated it was responsive to Sandostatin. (We did the right course of action.) His behaved in a very unusual way. (But we did everything right.) It was far more aggressive than typical and has taken over his body. There was nothing more they could do for him. (It's not our / my fault.) He looked me in the eyes and said, "I am sorry." And then he left. I am not sure if we ever saw him again. This was the world-renowned expert in neuroendocrine carcinoid whose assistant said to us at our last appointment before we left on our Michigan vacation. "Nothing dramatic would happen in two weeks." I never saw Bridget again but I wanted to tell her that I did consider a $20,000 ride across the pond in an emergency transport plane to be dramatic.

I have very little recollection of my reaction. We knew, of course, what Dr. Benson was going to say before he walked into the room. We had been waiting all night for the doctor to arrive to tell us the news that we already knew. But this was the process. Victor was calm. No anger. It is what it is. We took our cues from him. "I have had a good life," he said.

We didn't tweet in 2008 but the news spread like a wildfire and people started calling and visiting. I was beginning to panic. *How do I do this? How do I sit by my husband's bedside and wait for him to die? Who do I call? Is there a book for this? A Web site? Has someone written **Dying for Dummies**?*

After Dr. Benson left, the intensive care doctors began planning Victor's transport over to the new Prentice Women's hospital 16th floor. The terminal cancer ward. Then unexpectedly a group of women walked into the room. "We are your palliative care team," one of them said.

thing. You never got used to it, the idea of someone being gone. Just

I thought, *What the hell is a Palliative care team?* There were three of them. A particularly stylish woman was the leader. She was the only person not wearing doctor hospital clothes. She was colorful in her St. John knit suit with Taryn Rose shoes and a beautiful shawl that looked like it was imported from Asia. "I am Dr. Jamie Van Roenn and we will help you and your family with end-of-life care. Our goal is to make you as comfortable as possible and help you with pain management."

"His or mine?"

"Both." She was a straight talker. Calm. Did not dance around the question nobody else would answer. "It is not immediate, but if you live more than a month I would be surprised."

Dr. Van Roenn said, "Clear your calendar and take this time you have together, to enjoy each other. Sit with your wife alone and with each of your daughters. Your conversation goes like this. *Please forgive me; I forgive you; thank you; I love you;* and *goodbye.* We are here for you if you need anything. One of us will visit every day. Here is my cell phone number." Any conversation about hope or can't we try another treatment was cut off with a hatchet. "He is going to die," she said. "The opportunity to say goodbye is a gift."

And then it began. Three weeks of complete terror combined with pure joy. The wildfire of news burned out of control and people started coming. A

when you think it's reconciled, accepted, someone points it out to you, cousin from Los Angeles. College roommate from Boston. Summer friends from Texas. Relatives from Cincinnati. It was often too crowded in the room. They gave us a bigger room. The activity was numbing. The guard in the lobby stopped asking what room everyone was going to because he already knew. My friends rallied. One took my phone away and screened my calls and one created a website on *Lots of Helping Hands* where people could join the community. Victor and I made a post once a day so everyone could be part of the process. A schedule was created. No more visitors without an appointment. Open hours for our closest friends after five. Nobody before nine a.m. That was my time. Routine set in and we could sit back and enjoy.

Most nights I slept on the pullout couch so when Victor woke in middle of night I could be there. I set up speakers with my iPod and we listened to music. A lot of opera and the Beatles. He would say, "Let's check the website." And on the computer screen was an outpouring of love and memories. Stories from college. Pictures we'd never seen before. Messages of love and friendship. "Megatons of nostalgia," he would say. And we lived in the moment like we had never done before.

Dr. Van Roenn would stop by daily. After two weeks I said, "I am exhausted. I need to sleep."

She looked at me and said, "You have your whole life to sleep. You don't need to do it now."

At one point I broke down sobbing and said, "I can't do this anymore."

She pulled me out into the hall and said sternly, "Look, you are doing this as well as anybody I have ever seen. Don't stop now."

Victor didn't feel sorry for himself or express anger. He was every nurse's favorite patient. He enjoyed his last days of life. And so I did. We all did. Friends and family would come and go. My friends from work would stop by. We watched the Cubs while listening to Steve Goodman's "A Dying Cubs Fan's Last Request." I brought in wine and cheese for our guests. A cousin sent an oil painting to hang in his hospital room. We watched the Chicago to Mackinac race from his bed. We sang songs around my computer like it was a campfire.

And every morning we would watch the sunrise together. I would make coffee and he would sing "coffee for the sweetie" – a song that he sang for me every day of our married life as he delivered coffee to me in bed. Just the two of us. Life was good. It was one of the best times of our life together.

And then he died. And I am alone but not lonely. And I keep talking to him. *I forgive you, please forgive me, thank you, I love you* and *I am so happy that I got to say goodbye.*

And I wonder. What if we had that conversation and he didn't die? What if we planned three weeks a year to just enjoy life together? Or even one day.

"Life is eternal and love is immortal, and death is only a horizon; and

I forgive you. Please forgive me. Thank you. I love you. But not goodbye.

Clearing the Calendar

Lian Gouw

Steam from morning coffee
spirals around tasks concerning only me.
A contrast to the squares of my desk calendar
still filled with pencil notes of his appointments.

I take the small red square of rubber
from my drawer.
Move it across the pad, erasing
doctor's appointments, nurse's visits,
places to go, people to see,
business to take care of, things to talk about,
items to re-order, meals to cook.

Time moved a night between two days.
Dissolved necessities.
It is too late for things not done and words not
    spoken.

The squares are mostly empty now.
I take a pen and write in today's white space:
— *funeral.*

While Grieving

Peter D. Goodwin

Twice already
the neighbors have mowed their lawn
each time edging into my uncut yard,
as if to say, *it's time, past time.*

Amid the dead daffodils,
scraggly grasses, dandelions, buttercups
and weeds there are lots and lots
of tiny delicate violets.

She cried when I decapitated
the violets; and today,
on a beautiful spring afternoon
I too am crying.

The Colander

Peggy Muir

Feb 17, 2010

I just had a new top put on my kitchen counter. It looks great and there was not as much rot under and behind as expected so it was a cheaper and faster job than I had dreaded. I had to pull everything off shelves and out of drawers and now I am weeding, trying to divest of some of the clutter, some of the stuff. I am determined to get rid of stuff. There are tops without bottoms and bottoms without tops and cracked bowls and rusted cookie sheets and extra serving spoons and lots of mugs. I was a teacher and teachers get mugs as gifts; some of them have college names or cute sayings, some of them have historical quotes or famous faces. Some are handmade. Some can go.

And then there's the colander.

It's bright green enamelware and was bought, I'm pretty sure, in an import shop on 10th Street in Greenwich Village, on one of our early trips to New York. My first kitchen was bright brazen grass green so the colander matched (as did the walls and the dishtowels). It has lived in every house

pers the o'er fraught heart and bids it break." William Shakespeare we've had, usually right out in the open by the sink. One of the visual icons of the household. It has been used almost daily for washing salad.

Salad is a food group in our house. The green colander has briefly housed romaine and *reine de glace* and arugula and spinach and red leaf and mustard and Black-Seeded Simpson and nasturtium leaves and all the other kinds of salad greens I grow in my garden out back. Every soft summer twilight in my memory I am walking through the garden, filling the colander with selected leaves and bringing the greens in to be washed. Bryce comes in from his shop for whatever we are eating with salad. The daily round.

When Seth was tiny, I had the colander on a hook by the sink and it fell on him while I was giving him a kitchen sink bath. Bryce in fury pitched it across the kitchen; that may be when it got chipped.

Now it's missing a handle and, where it's chipped, there's visible rust. I have a newer mesh colander with a long handle that enables it to perch efficiently across the sink. The green colander isn't used much anymore, except to hold the new colander, and my kitchen isn't green anymore.

And my husband is gone.

I put the colander in the box for the recycling barn. But I haven't taken it yet and wonder if I will. It was bright green when my marriage was new and green. It was part of our Salad Days. I think bizarrely

that an atom of my husband's being may adhere to
it. If I get rid of the colander, am I getting rid of more
of him? Or can I hold the salad memories in me?

April 2012 –
　　I still have the colander and smile when I see it.

The Aging Widow Understands
Patricia L. Goodman

An adolescent house finch perches
on my window feeder, looking like
he was out too late with an older brother.

His untidy head feathers are slimed,
stuck together, the rest of him rumpled,
as if he just tumbled from the nest.

Chubby physique too inflexible
to bend into the seed ports,
he sits with a puzzled stare,

not sure what to do with
his new body/his new life.

"Hell! I Forgot Red!"

Sheryl L. Nelms

she
said

leaning over
the seat

so I did
a U-Turn
on 13th Street

and went
back

to Lakeview Crematory
still crowded
from the
service

for her husband's
silver urn
of ash

Where's Grampa?

Sharon Ellison

That's what my three-year-old grandson asked when he walked into my den the day after my husband died. My son and daughter-in-love had explained about Grampa's death to their six-year-old son, but Liam was too young for explanations... they thought.

So, in he walked with his usual big smile, stopped in the middle of the den, looked around with a puzzled expression and said, "Where's Grampa?" His Grampa had, for the last thirteen months, either been in his recliner or in a hospital bed in our den.

Think of those old E. F. Hutton commercials. That's the kind of moment his parents and I had. We each stood stunned while Liam looked expectantly from one of us to the other, waiting for his answer.

Taking a deep breath, I leaned toward him, smiled and said, "Liam, Grampa went to see Jesus."

Liam's smile returned. "Grampa went to see Jesus?"

"Yes," I responded quietly as I continued to smile. He never noticed my tears.

"Oh! Okay!" came his happy reply as he headed straight for the toy box.

His parents and I looked at each other, relieved. We know Liam has no idea yet what my answer really means; however, he has heard stories about Jesus both at home and in Sunday school and he knows that being with Jesus is a good place to be.

One day Liam will understand completely, but until that time, I will always be grateful that God gave me the right words at the right time.

First Christmas Again
Patricia Wellingham-Jones

She bolted from the house,
from turkey gravy she was stirring,
from guests with wine glasses
tilted to their lips,
from her new step-daughter's family.

In the slight protection of the eaves
she opened her mouth, released
into rain the wail that had built
through an endless round of hosting.
Bent from the waist, she roared out sobs
she'd swallowed all day.

Heedless of her hairdo
she stepped away from shelter

land of the dead and the bridge is love, the only survival, the only

into storm, tipped her head back,
let rain wash down her cheeks
with tears.

Returning through a distant door
she splashed cold water on red, swollen eyes,
dragged a comb through flattened hair,
freshened makeup. Pinning a smile
on still-trembling lips, she rejoined the group

apologizing to nobody,
including her husband
of a few months,
for missing the one
no longer there.

Haiku Sequence

Karen O'Leary

face down
in the river
dreams die

water gushes
over the hill
a widow's tears

the river flows
her life without him
stands still

stones

Meta E. Lee

my trembling fingers trace contours of simple stones
    prominent jutting spikes
        size/shape of vertebra or a newborn's thumb
        beige/gray some nearly white
        no lingering fragrance of the earth

stones that bordered the pathway where he
    parked his car
        laughed when the dog pawed them in search
            of a phantom bone
        mock-scolded when i drove too close and
            pebbles flew

i grace his grave with these stones
    oddly warm from sweet/fresh tears
    on this sunless day

i whisper now
    they'll be your sentinel
    honoring your final day
    witness to my loneliness

The Huntress

Carol McAdoo Rehme

Decide the time is ripe.

After all, you are. Ripe, that is. Ripe for the pickin'. Perhaps even over-ripe. Isn't that the point? Just like fruit. Anything much beyond is only good for a breakfast blender concoction or – in the case of apples – stewed, poached, or pureed and spread in a thin layer to be dehydrated into leather.

Come to think of it, the aging skin across your collarbone and chest is beginning to look leathery. And your knees are starting to sag from the weight of their wrinkles. And, what, is that an actual pimple? At your age? Hormones, you sigh.

Yes, now is definitely the time. Time to look for a man. Again. Even though you swore you could never love another, would never want another, would never need another man.

Early on, you heated a can of Campbell's and, forgetting, divided it between two bowls. When you realized your mistake, you poured them in the sink and ran cold water until the last chunk of chicken and the remaining half noodle slithered down the drain. Your sobs drowned out the grind and growl of the garbage disposal.

Yet you knew you had to eat. So you tried taking your meals at the Country Kitchen, but their sign lied. Home cookin' shouldn't be as tasteless and dry as pricey funeral cards. Wendy's dollar menu worked: a salad or a bowl of chili and you could even pick it up at the drive-through. A meal-for-one. And, of course, a real value with extra packets of saltines and dressing. No need to change out of your sweats, comb your hair, or do your face.

Or sit at a table, a woman alone.

No wonder you'd drifted into The Pack – even though you swore you never would. Remember when the two of you raised your brows and rolled your eyes each time the five gals appeared – *en masse* – at the main street McDonald's for morning coffee? They came mostly for the free refills and an opportunity to read the weekend newspaper strewn across the booths. Or so they said.

As tight-faced as they are tight-fisted, the widow women prowl local events to see and be seen. To fill the hours. And you are the latest inductee to their club, following them from retirement gala drop-ins to church revivals; from lectures at the community college to wedding receptions; from park concerts to grand openings of (take your pick) floral shops, branch banks, boutiques and gas stations, where they sniff out the refreshment table hoping all four major food groups will be represented.

Which is how you found yourself frequenting funerals. Who knew small-town funerals would

many years with a good wife and then outlived her. If two people love

become the social highlight of your week? Of course you were acquainted with the deceased – most of them. Or someone in The Pack probably was. Or, perhaps not. Nevertheless, in addition to the eats afterwards, it was another opportunity to dress to the nines and accessorize. You never knew who you'd meet.

Divorced friends-of-friends.

Widowers.

Bachelor uncles.

Oh, sure, at your age single women seem to far outnumber the available men. And you repeat among yourselves the stale line that all you really need is one good man to share between you. The only requirement? He must be willing to drive at night.

You join in the laughter and nod, swallowing the urge to confess the hollowness of both house and heart each time you walk in the door after an evening out. Those nights when you're full to overflowing, eager to share your rapture over the sweet strains of Beethoven's *Fifth* that filled the rotunda at the open-air concert. And your timid questions about the visiting professor's long-winded delivery on the chitinous exoskeletons of aquatic arthropods. And your uncertainty about opening another account at the new bank.

And to gossip with him about: the school board's decision to fire the superintendent...the Babcocks' separation on the heels of their fortieth anniversary

cruise...the tattooed attendant at the gas station...
the rate increase in the water bill...Rita Ellsworth's
latest hair color...the pastor's untimely resignation...

But his coffee-stained recliner sits eerily unoccu-
pied, a mute witness to the label that advertises
your singleness and threatens to strangle you.
Widow.

And, of course, you never confess to the girls
how much you miss his toasty shins to sandwich
your icy toes. Or the comfort of a solid frame to roll
against after an unsettling dream. Or the morning
nuzzle of a whiskered face against the back of your
neck. Or your longings for a...

flirtatious pat on the fanny;
breathy nibble on your ear;
lingering, full-body hug;
restless, kneading grope;
ohhhh...dear...God.

Problem is, when you finally do track down a
man-with-possibility and you're traveling as one
with The Pack, complications arise before you can
even get close enough to savor his aftershave.
While you're still mining your over-sized handbag
for a crimson lipstick – Bold Seduction – among the
packets of croutons, Italian lite, and finely powdered
saltines...complementary ink pens from the insur-
ance agency and the health fair tumble to the floor
and your hangnail snags on a crumpled Kleenex
and drags it, too, from the catacombs of your

"The continuity of being is lacerated; the settled course of sentiment

purse... Why, by then, the hungry predators already surround their prey and tempt him with smiles.

Tease him with flattery.

Badger him with requests for household repairs.

Bait him with invitations for outings.

Lure him with offers of home-cooked meals.

But you? You retreat. Again. After all, you reason, no man is worth losing a girlfriend over. You recall the often-shared joke about girlfriends being vital: With menopausal memory problems, it takes all of you together just to finish a sentence!

A grimace twists your mouth. *No wonder*, you think. *We always know what the other wants to say because there's not an original thought among us.*

You're hit by an overpowering urge to tuck your tail between your legs and hightail it out of there. Away from the aimless social life. Away from all-too-knowing eyes. Away from The Pack.

Ah. Now that's an original thought. Going solo, without the comfort − and competition − of the others. So, you've come full circle, haven't you? Back to the urge to hunt alone and bag your buck. A heart-healing grin sneaks across your face as you think, *Now, that's something he would've said.*

But you know The Pack will accuse you of poaching. Girlfriends rank higher than male com-panionship...right?

You recall a slide show at the college's "Who's Who in Greek Legend" lecture: a bare-breasted Atalanta whose story charmed you. The armed huntress ridded herself of unwanted suitors by

and action is stopped; and life stands suspended and motionless."

proclaiming she could be won only by the man who out-paced her.

"Wife and bed," she declared, "shall be given as prize unto the swift – but death be the reward of those who lag."

You laughed during the race scenes as man after handsome man fell by the wayside. Except for that gorgeous hunk Melanion. The clever fellow tossed golden apples backwards in his tracks, tempting beautiful Atalanta to slow and pick them up.

Why, *Atalanta chased him until he caught her!* you think. *How clever of her.*

And you plan your own ambush.

You pose before the "skinny" mirror on the back of your bedroom door. The mirror that gives you a boost of self-confidence while it subtracts ten pounds from your fat clothes.

You test-drive your smiles. Quick and flirtatious. Heavy-lidded and mysterious. Wide-eyed and innocent. Slow and seductive.

You step back for a full-length inventory and frown. You made friends with elastic waistbands years ago. Hmmm. The gym, perhaps? Then Atalanta's own full-bodied curves flash across your memory, immediately crowded out by the Community Center's standard fare of paunches, beer-bellies and suspenders.

Leaning in, you finger-flatten the part in your hair and inspect your roots. A touch-up, you wonder? Huh. You can get as accurate a reflection in the sea of bobbing bald pates and wispy comb-overs that shine at every concert down at the Rialto.

You bare your teeth like a horse at auction. Maybe one of those new whitening toothpastes? And you picture the church's monthly potluck with its side menu of dentures, partials, gold fillings, tobacco stains...

You pause. You look again, probing the mirror for flaws. Instead, you discover a remarkably attractive, amazingly beguiling, startlingly well-preserved woman gazing back.

Ready for the chase and ripe for the picking. A golden apple of temptation.

Widow

Joy Gaines-Friedler

I've learned to put salt in the softener, to pay
the bills with no reluctance. I've learned
to fill the empty sections on the calendar.
I can phone a roofer should I need to,
take the car in for alignment. Every day I wake
to the same light through our bedroom window
to the same absence, to the same alarm.

The room where you died a month ago
Patricia Wellingham-Jones

Your desk is gone, file cabinet
and hospital bed given away.
Even the bedside commode
found a home.

I threw the corner windows wide,
let the north wind scour the walls,
burned cedar incense
to cleanse and freshen the space.

Now a chair and floor lamp stand
on a flowered carpet.
A new bed with new linens
hugs the far wall.

Your cat settles in that room
as if your scent still holds her fast.
I lie beside her, tears streaking my face,
stroke her soft fur.

Any Other Name

K. Marguerite Caronna

The literature tells you that part of grieving is re-establishing your identity. With the unexpected passing of my husband, I have found myself needing to come to terms with new titles. What to call my husband? He's not my ex-husband – everyone seems to have a few of those around. Dearly departed? For where? I lost my husband? I did that once – in Costco. My late husband? Since he passed suddenly pre-maturely, this seems wrong. Early seems more appropriate than late. Ahead of schedule for his appointment in Samarra.

And then, I can't wrap my mind around calling myself a widow. What is it with widows? Widows are somehow suspect, stigmatized in our culture. There are black widows, brown widows, and opportunistic merry widows. There's no Merry Widower waltz. Widower conjures up winsome men standing at doors accepting casseroles from consoling ladies. What man ever delivered comfort food to a widow? His wife would smack him! In some cultures, widows are killed or shunned. Widow Pritchard, the witch who lives in a shack in the forest, is known to cavort with the devil at midnight.

Who can blame her? What else do you do after you've had a bottle of wine and watched every *Law and Order* rerun to fill your evenings?

In *The Postman Always Rings Twice*, a cop says, "Accidental death, ha! Did you get a look at the widow?" His knowing glance at Lana Turner says it all: *hubba-hubba.* When did anyone ever say, "Hey, get a load'a that widower!" It's, "the widower, poor fella." Anna Nicole Smith was a widow and she ended up in court. A "rich widow" lights a gleam in the eye. Impoverished widows taking in boarders only evoke pity.

I'm not single, yet I'm not married. In some ways I'm freer than I've ever been, yet tethered to the past by sweet and painful memories. Grief ambushes me in the strangest ways: the light of the sun on a distant tree, a breeze against my cheek. A picture at the back of a drawer. I search for myself in a morass of emotions, putting one foot in front of the other, sometimes hour by hour, day by day. I suppose eventually, I'll stop being a closet widow – did you think of spiders just then? And someday, so I'm told, maybe even waltz again.

Afterword

Barbara Darnall

Our daughter called from the hospital, saying only,
"Hurry," but you couldn't wait, and so you began
your last journey without me, to a place with no
    more pain
and gasping breath, only fresh air, sunlight, and
    everlasting
joy. I sat by your bed, holding your hand, stroking
    your arm,
not yet able to say my last goodbye. For a moment
I wanted to go with you, leave behind
    heartbreaking loss
and all the empty days I knew would be ahead. But I
heard a sobbing grandson, saw a bereft daughter,
    grieving son,
loved ones all – my family, who needed me and
    for whom
I needed to be strong. I remember following your
    body
out into the blazing sunlight of a spring morning I
    could not see
for the tears. For the first time in forty-six years I
    was one, alone,
and not one-half of two.

vert to the past: no man is as good as his wife says her first husband

A Widow Looks Back

Marian Veverka

I used to say *you're going to drive me crazy*
You used to say I'd be the death of you
Maybe I was, you snuck away so easy
From the couch, watching the evening news
While I washed the dishes, never realized
The news was going on without you, I turned
To change the channel, you looked so peaceful
It took a moment or two before I learned…
Six seasons passed, yet still I feel your presence
So often I will pause, believing that I've heard
You clear your throat, your cough and then your sigh
We watched our faces turn wrinkled, our children grow
And enter their own histories. The trees, grown high
but beautiful, today they are filling up with snow

Time – that old buzzard – sits and waits. Going
    first is the lucky one.
Saying goodbye to you, my love, was the hardest
    thing I've ever done.

In a Fix

Kathe Campbell

Honey, when you have a minute would you go downstairs and up the temperature on the hot water tank? Oh, and there's a leaky pipe under the bathroom sink, a hinge on the hay room door fell off, and one of the ATV's has a low tire. Similar requests ring through the ages, as in my own fifty-three-year marriage.

Pops always had a minute, for all was lovingly repaired by a man who knew how to keep a household and farm in fine fettle. He also made sure our children and I knew how to handle simpler electrical and plumbing nightmares without seeing stars or finding ourselves mired in toilet water.

Although I've always been capable of wielding a hammer or turning a screw to fix minor mishaps, the worst days of my life arrived somberly and darkly. An uncertain cloud hung over our family, watching Pop suffer dreadful complications from rheumatoid arthritis. No longer would we find him at his work bench sharpening chainsaws, building a pulley system for bird feeders, or under a vehicle

never really heals the tragic memory of such a great loss, but we carry

changing oil. I now had a dreary spring to contemplate going it alone.

As the new dowager of Broken Tree Ranch, the weather and I became kindred spirits on this shivery mountain with its cold rains. Realizing God never made anything as resilient as the human spirit, I prayed silently beneath beads of sweat... "This one-armed lady is trusting in your wisdom on this crazy journey, Lord."

I pondered being capable of honoring Pop's last words, "...and take good care of our ranch, Hon." How dare he leave me in such a fix!

The heavy new hook on my prosthesis had this old prune listing as my dog eagerly ushered our way to morning chores. Would I remember all Pops had taught me about proper care of the animals and equipment? Could I load the rifle and put a shot over the head of some thieving varmint without shooting my foot off? Bent on lifting my burden with his wide smile and love-light shining, my pup's warm tongue slurped cold tears as I knelt to cut open a bale.

I made a list of the large, unwieldy stuff I would have no use for. Pops rarely threw anything away, so a mad hunt began matching ancient titles and instruction books with all that I advertised in our newspaper. After a successful sale, I spent the remainder of the summer floundering in piles of paperwork. I turned our business over to a daughter's capable hands, dealt with the VA, Medicare,

on, because we have to, because our loved one would want us to, and be-

endless insurance policies, and revamped my filing cabinets and den. It was the last time I recognized my signatures due to my own crippling rheumatoid.

Lovely autumn days arrived for rides up the mountain and fence inspection around my acres, but despite constant charging, the old ATV battery conked. What could be so hard? Surely a new battery will go in smoothly if I remember how I took the old one out. So I replaced the old with new, proudly installed single-handedly. Miserably slow with every project, my heart zinged whenever engines roared to a lively start. From that day on I ably ordered things like a new starter solenoid for the Bobcat that cleaned barn and plowed snow. Installing most of them lickety-split, I whispered... "Are you watching me, Pops?"

After claiming the finest of Pop's cherished cache for their own garages, the day came when the children and I set a thousand and one items out on benches and tables. A set of metrics here, Dremels there, for if Pops had one, there were always two and three of every handyman gadget invented. Another ad went in the newspaper, and at dawn on a Friday morning everybody and their brother banded like sheep outside my gate waiting to exploit my stuff. Pop's beloved tools and parts sold like hotcakes leaving a lump in my throat, for much had helped build our homes and repair play toys.

Peace and quiet at last as the walls shuddered and heaved a sigh. The squirrels were put out, but this lovely log building with its tack room, hay room, and bunkhouse looked handsome with Pop's favorite treasures hanging orderly. There was finally room for why garages were invented, and I stood mesmerized, mumbling my thoughts... "You taught us well, Pops, and I forgive you for leaving me in such a fix."

Gone? Not Really.

Gail Denham

Commemorate a life. Take your time.
Spend a day, two weeks, four months
to consider this person. Maybe
that's not enough. Perhaps it takes
two or three years, or a lifetime.

Memories dart in at odd times. That's his scent.
Under the window, the chair sits empty,
covered with a blue and red afghan. A breeze
moves the rocker. No one's there, but it's full
of the weight of that funny, dear man.

A car passes. You glimpse a tanned face
under dark curly hair, like his, once.
His fishing reel turns up under the desk
with a battered green hat. You move a pillow
and find one worn winter sock.

The phone rings, and you expect...what?

Will it ever end? No. Why should it?

Folks so close don't leave. They're
near. They populate our thoughts.
Though blurred by time, we see their faces.
Our memory kicks in. Laughter
echoes. A song tickles our heart.

We can't lose them. They're part of who we are —
who we have been – what we will become.

Comfort wraps around your shoulders with the bright
afghan. Your feet start the rocker. You settle in for
　　a remembrance visit.

June Rose Dowis

the moment between
waking and remembering
a widow's first morn

New Perspective

Alice King Greenwood

I'm unaccustomed to a silent house
where I don't hear your voice call my name.
I see your cluttered desk, the books you browsed
left lying undisturbed. They still retain
the soft scent of your touch. Your empty chair
speaks muted evidence of solemn times
you spent engrossed in meditative prayer,
or times when memories made laughter climb
into your face. You sing a soundless song,
a quiet air. The poignant potpourri
of all you are, you give to me. I long
to hold this moment of epiphany:
Our love enfolds what loneliness devours;
the things you leave behind are always ours.

Ripples

Kehaunani Hubbard

"Are we lost?" She tried to keep her voice from quivering.

"I'm following the MapQuest directions, so we should be okay." It was just past ten in the morning and already sweat dribbled down the valley of my back. "I think that was it, let me just turn around."

The government-issued "Harpeth River State Park" sign marked the trailhead in a meadow of flowers. We were in search of Hidden Lake and the trail guide said it was here. I wanted to explore the areas surrounding our new home in Nashville, Tennessee.

We followed the mowed trail through the meadow, watching grasshoppers prance up the path. My six-year-old daughter, who carried her father's hunched shoulders, squatted on the path, studied a butterfly sunbathing on some grass.

"Don't touch the wings."

"I'm not, I'm just looking."

"Well, don't look with your fingers."

A fluorescent-tailed dragonfly zoomed past us, stealing Savannah's attention and in the next breath she was in hot pursuit. Immediately upon entering the forest I smelled deep, wet earth and sniffing like a hound dog I followed my nose until I discovered a river the color of muddy tea.

"Are we there yet? I am soooooo hot! Where is the..." She stumbled off after another grasshopper.

Are we there yet indeed. This question had been bouncing in my brain, zigging and zagging between my frontal lobes. *I don't know where I am, my lovely daughter, I am in a freefall with the burden of a new widow's grief and a single mother's duties.*

All I knew is why I ran away to Tennessee. Los Angeles held too many memories of my husband's three-year odyssey with brain cancer; California reeked of pain. The hospital had only been six minutes from the house and I couldn't drive home without passing it. The beach was our family outing place; I couldn't go there either. Even the grocery store conjured up tears. Everywhere I went Los Angeles pointed out the fact that my husband was dead and that Savannah would grow up without a father. Nashville offered a chance for a new start.

The air was thick and wet as we continued along the forested path for another mile. The trail abruptly turned right taking us even further away from the Harpeth River. *How far away can a lake be from a river? How much longer would I sweat?* As we came down a slight hill we were treated to the splendor of Hidden Lake. Our goal for the walk was to discover this lake, but the name had eluded us until we marveled at the water below us. Immediately I felt a presence of calmness come over me. Steep walls of limestone a hundred feet high embraced the water. The tiny lake was the length and width of half a football field. A sparse forest stood sentry above it. There was a tiny rocky beach where Savannah promptly directed her feet. She discovered a frog and began jumping with excitement herself. There was a large cracked tree limb jutting into the calm waters, which claimed the rest of her attention. With the dexterity that only fearless children carry, she began balancing on the log without concern for a wet fall.

Watching her bounce from one distraction to the next brought a tearful smile to my lips. She had weathered her father's death quite well, staying present in the moments since his death. I, on the other hand, had felt nothing but burdened with my sadness, carrying it around with me like chain mail. All that weight kept me away from whatever joy was happening around me. My grief was costing me pleasures I could be experiencing with Savannah. Watching her play jolted a revelation: life didn't have to be so tragic. Life could also be magical, if I could only sit in the present of the now and not wander about in the past. But moving forward seemed impossible and improbable. My grief was still too raw, the memories too sharp.

"Mom, watch!" Everything with young children seems to end with an exclamation mark. She hoisted a large rock and *kerthump*...it spread concentric circles in the lake. I squatted next to the log, keeping a watchful eye on Savannah's exuberant activity. More stones were thrown into the lake, creating more ripples. I watched the circles fade away. As each ripple moved away from its inception, the rings became wider until they disappeared. I could try to do that. I wanted to do that. Let the fresh agony have its way with me, but also allow it to move away as feelings are wont to do. Don't hold on to the pain, let it wash over me so I can be present for what the next moment might bring. And the next moment might be another flush of sadness but it might also be a sparkle of joy that my daughter held out for me to embrace.

Helen Ruggieri

after the holiday
the wishbone is ready but
no one to wish with

the clichés that cause the trouble. To lose someone you love is to alter

The Coffee Maker

Penny Righthand

Every morning the sound of the coffee grinding mixed with the smell of the freshly ground beans was their wake up call; a rousing welcome to the new day. The perfect Panasonic coffee maker came with him into their relationship and lived with them throughout. He had one at his house, and after several months, an identical one showed up at her house. She wasn't sure where he'd got it since they were no longer being sold in this country. But there it was, on her kitchen counter. And there it stayed for 21 years.

Sometime after he died, her coffee maker broke. Well, actually not the whole thing; just the bean basket. With a certain sadness and resignation, she climbed on a stool in her kitchen to find the old coffee filter system she had used before Richard and the Panasonic had come into her life. As she reached into the cupboard, she saw there was another identical bean basket way up in the back. And next to it, several more boxes stacked behind one another with miscellaneous parts of Panasonic coffee makers. She started moving them down from the shelves, one after another, watching the collection accumulate exponentially on her counter and the floor. Each box contained several different replacement parts. In total, when she organized them and began putting them together, there were nineteen complete Panasonic coffee makers, and seventeen additional parts.

She thought about the storage unit she paid for monthly, filled with thousands of his CDs on spindles, 21 cartons of crystal boxes, hundreds of boxes of his books, multiple mid-century chairs and couches, antique works of art, boxes of staplers of every make and style, and paperclips in interesting geometric shapes that didn't hold any papers together. There was at least one carton of photo postcards of Niagara Falls from the 1950s, with strangers' honeymoon notes on the backs. He had collected everything to excess. She knew this. So why was she surprised to find nineteen identical coffee makers?!

She remembered how she'd mocked him when he'd shown up at her house with twenty boxes of Kleenex and ten flats of Crystal Geyser (unflavored for her); how she'd chastised him like a child bringing a dirty rock collection into the house, for cluttering her condo with these things she had no room for; how he'd carried them back down to his car and kept them hidden in the trunk so whenever she needed them, they magically appeared.

She felt sad and foolish for having not appreciated these as love offerings, despite their coming, perhaps, from some inexplicable need to have enough. He had tried to take good care of her, and, in fact, had. But only now, now that she realized she could continue to awaken to the smell of freshly ground coffee beans, probably indefinitely, did she realize how lucky she'd been; how grateful she was for his love, no matter how it had been expressed.

The Widow

Villisca Cemetery, Villisca, Iowa
Laura Madeline Wiseman

Guarded by a low stone wall, the family plot
marks his lineage, MOTHER, FATHER, etc.
in the space of a sandbox. Claiming dead center,
his joint monument stands erect and several feet
    taller
than the family, while his wife remains a blank
raised box after the dash, as if she did away
with the vows, the blizzard's mean snarl and bite,
and chose not to lie down and be buried beside
    this man.

Widower

Milton P. Ehrlich

My mate of sixty years left this world before me.
She predicted I'd never change the sheets,
or even know where to find them.

Standing before the washer-dryer
the soaps all seem strange; I'll never find the lint
that must be wheedled from a trap.

I used to drop my socks and fling them in a basket.
Yawning, half-asleep, I'd reach into a dresser
   drawer
for matching socks and folded underwear.

Flannel pajamas vanished in the spring
replaced by lightweight cotton nightwear.
She lined up shirts and pants and chose a
   matching tie.

She did the shopping, cleaning, laundry and
   sprayed
the evening primrose creating the aura of a
   rainbow.
Protective of my sleep, her bountiful breasts
nursed our crying kids at night.

All I did was run around on tennis courts
   whenever I wasn't working.

Mornings, she sang Portuguese *fado* in the shower.
Evenings, we'd bang on kitchen pots and she'd
   perform,
undulating like an incarnation of a cosmic dancing
   Shiva.

Her sense of touch had sources in the esoteric
as analeptic as any healing touch at Lourdes.

And if and when I got the itch and felt the need for
   intimacy
I'd cuddle up and we'd merge seamlessly,
smooth as the velvety sheen of drawn butter on a
   lobster tail.

Our souls would smile self-consciously,
   whispering
words of the unsayable said.

A celebrant of being present, she breathed life
   into my air
with a whir and whirl of joy, watching over me
like a beady-eyed benevolent white dove.

Who will fly over me now?

The Crossing

Judy Lee Green

Lonesome bore down on Mama when Daddy died like a Kentucky coal train on the mainline to Bull Run. Forty-six years of memories flashed before her like a long line of freight cars, made her dizzy with remembering, thundered like ghosts from the past. With her crossing guard arms folded across her chest, teary eyes blinked like red warning lights flashing, grief sounded as loud as bells clanging, her moaning like a train whistle on a dismal night. Like a hobo grabbing a freight car, she seized the memories passing at breakneck speed and held on before they could vanish beyond the crossing.

Blind Dates

Stella Rimmer

A few days after my husband died one of my aunts came to visit me. She threw her arms around me, sobbing, and said "Don't worry, darling, I'll find someone else for you." This was not what I wanted to hear at that particular time – but in her own naïve and endearing manner I knew she meant well. Months later, remaining true to her word, she phoned and said she had arranged for me to meet a "lovely man" and out of respect for her good intentions, and somewhat misguidedly, I agreed.

On the dreaded day I got dressed, acutely conscious of my husband staring out at me from the photograph on my bedside table, and wondered what the hell I was doing. But I felt compelled to honour the promise I had made to my aunt and made my way to the designated restaurant. Mr. Mystery Man had told me on the phone that he would be holding a red rose so that I could identify him and this was my first warning signal. But I had ignored it and instead found myself standing in the entrance of the restaurant – a forty-one-year-old

Thomas ~§~ "For it was not into my ear you whispered, but into my

mature and experienced woman – quivering like a bowl of jello, wanting to run. As I turned to leave I felt a tap on my shoulder and there stood Mr. Mystery Man complete with red rose – and it was too late. I now have no idea what this man looked like, which is probably a fair indication that I certainly felt no chemistry towards him whatsoever. What I do remember – vividly – is him suddenly standing up in the middle of the meal announcing that he had written a love poem for me, which he then proceeded to recite – loudly! *God is punishing me*, I thought. Not surprisingly I recall little else of that evening other than making a silent vow never to agree to a blind date again!

How quickly we forget – and I am, after all, only human. So some time later when a cousin phoned to say she knew a divorced man who had seen me at a recent family wedding and asked her for my phone number, I gave her permission to pass it on. What was I thinking? I guess family pressure can be a powerful tool and so it was that I found myself a week later opening the door to Blind Date No. 2. The first thing he said to me was "Hope you don't mind walking...I'm out of work right now and haven't got much money." Slightly aghast at this introduction but trying to remain open-minded I told myself that at least he was being honest and assumed that we were probably just going to walk to the top of my road where there was a choice of many restaurants and cafés. Some five hours later,

heart. It was not my lips you kissed, but my soul." Judy Garland ~§~

as I sat in my kitchen soaking my sore and blistered feet, I wondered why I had not, before leaving home with him, changed my three-inch heels for some flats! But how was I to know that he was intent on taking me to a particular café he liked because of their "excellent coffee" or that it was situated in the heart of London, an hour and a half walk from my home in the suburbs!

Surely becoming a widow at the age of 41 had not made me less intelligent, nor less discerning. If anything, it had transformed me into a much stronger person who held down an important job in a legal firm, enjoying the company of many good friends and enabling me to make some important decisions relative to my home and daughters along the way. Of course I felt lonely at times but I was not alone – and yet the ability to say *no* to the matchmakers of my family circle was sadly lacking. These were the things that I mused on while I sat opposite the man who spent most of the evening explaining his late wife's recipes for chopped liver and chicken soup and then yet another who showed me several photographs of his beloved, extolling her excellent taste in clothes. Maybe it was something to do with the adage of "hope springs eternal" and subconsciously I thought that perhaps there was another special someone out there for me. But if there was, he certainly didn't show up on any of my blind dates and eventually I did learn to say *no*.

"A widow has two duties of a contradictory nature – she is a mother,

I continued to say *no* until I arrived in Israel a couple of years ago. "You should sign up for JDate," my son-in-law said.

"You have to be joking," I replied. But he was definitely not joking and proceeded to tell me about several people he knew who had found this an excellent way to meet people and that indeed his own sister had met her fiancé via this route. I should mention that my son-in-law is a well known speaker both in Israel and internationally. He is an extremely convincing speaker and so, not surprisingly, I found myself sitting next to him at his computer logging into JDate.com and typing up my profile.

I am somewhat embarrassed to admit that half an hour later, when he checked out the site to make sure that my registration had gone through correctly, I felt just a tad excited when he told me that I had already received several responses. There I was, a seventy-two-year-old teenager, responding to this new "computer speak" of icons with silly smiley faces winking at me from the screen and reading messages from men in their late 30's to mid-70's.

The mid-30's group somewhat baffled and worried me but it was so bizarre that simply out of curiosity I felt compelled to read their profiles and even, for a while, exchanged emails with some of them. A few were strangely insistent on wanting to make arrangements to meet up with me and had I been several years younger I probably would have done so. Instead I eventually plucked up the nerve to meet up with one or two of the more age-appropriate men. They say "age doesn't matter" and after talking to a few of them face to face I realized that this was probably true because they were no more – and possibly less – on my mental wavelength than the younger ones. The two most memorable ones were the Card Player and the Ice Cream Man.

Fifteen minutes into my meeting with the Card Player, he asked if I played Bridge. When I jokingly told him that I didn't even play Snap and that I really had never enjoyed playing any card games at all, his jaw visibly dropped. He looked at me as though he was confronting some kind of alien and a few minutes later, after announcing that he was really looking for a new Bridge partner and probably would not contact me again, we said our goodbyes!

Mr. Ice Cream Man's attitude was a little more congenial, despite the absurdity of the venue. He asked me to meet him at MacDonalds where his first words to me were "I love ice cream – I hope you do, too." Well, yes, I do actually love ice cream – but whatever happened to taking a girl for a meal, or at the very least a glass of wine? Anyone who knows me will tell you that I am not the slightest bit mercenary – but if you're going to buy me an ice cream on a first date, at least splash out a little and order one of those chocolate fudge concoctions rather than a single scoop of vanilla in a wafer cone! However, surprisingly, apart from that, this man's conversation was reasonably stimulating and I was just about getting to the point where I could overlook the ice cream fiasco when he suddenly asked if I would spend the night with him at his apartment. What I really felt like saying was "Sorry – but it takes more than an ice cream cone to get me into bed with someone!" Instead, like an inexperienced bashful virgin, I mumbled something about having to get home early…and that was my last and final JDate.

The following day I logged on, cancelled my membership and finally was able to have a good laugh at myself and at all the ridiculous encounters I had experienced along the road of widowhood. So now, still alone at 73, I am eternally grateful for the crazy, passionate relationships I enjoyed before settling down and even more grateful that I eventually married my childhood sweetheart because I am only too aware that not everyone is fortunate enough to find a soulmate. You never know, that next special someone may still turn up one day – but I'm confident that it won't be as the result of a blind date!

Soaked into that room

Patricia Wellingham-Jones

His years soaked into that back room
licked the faded wallpaper
seeped into the rug.
The rump-sprung chair
carried the scent of him
and the musty smell of a thousand books.
A lifetime of evenings
then later full days
of reading under the old brass lamp
have soaked his presence so deep
we still feel him there
when we open the door.

Vere ~§~ "'Widow' is a harsh and hurtful word. It comes from the San-

Because We Kept the Trees
Carol Faulkner Peck

They thanked us, scattering desiccated limbs
Across the lawn, where over time the grass
Crept away to neighboring sunnier yards.
Green moss crept in, covered muddy earth,
Snuggled against protruding, gnarly roots.

Because we kept the ever-burgeoning trees,
They thanked us with profusion of summer leaves
That shaded sunny beds to silence . . .
Vegetables, flowers, abundance of butterflies
Are nothing but echoing memories.

Because we kept these tall, tenacious trees,
I now sit in your chair and travel through
The window to the pulsing poplars, maples . . .
Thanking each for keeping me inside
The world of gold that was, that is, to come.

From Bride to Widow

A Memoir of Love

                                                        CJ Heck

I remember so clearly the worst day of my life. It was on September 13, 1969. Actually, there were more days than just that one, but that's the one day I can talk about, at least for right now.

I was living at my childhood home in Ohio with my parents at the time. I had married my high school sweetheart, Doug Kempf, in January of 1969, and though in our hearts we were still newlyweds, Uncle Sam had other plans for Doug. In May, the Army sent him to Vietnam, where he wore a very different hat. In Vietnam, he was a combat medic: SP4; RA; HHC, 4th BN, 12th INF, 199th LIB.

Doug and I shared a wonderful life from January to May, before he went to Vietnam. We were military-poor and living in a trailer on base at Ft. Bragg in Fayetteville, North Carolina, but we didn't care. We were together and we were happy. There we loved and laughed and planned our future for when he returned. We had decided we wanted an old Victorian with lots of bedrooms, oak woodwork

~§~ *"WIDOW, n. A pathetic figure that the Christian world has*

and wainscoting, and a huge kitchen, because we loved entertaining family and friends. It would also have to have a large front porch with a wooden swing so we could watch thunderstorms and cuddle.

We decided three children would be perfect – two boys and a girl. The boys would be tall and handsome with their daddy's bowed legs – legs that loved to dance – and Doug's zany sense of humor, and that same infectious laugh. They would grow up to be good men who were looked up to for their strength of character. Smart, like their father, they would someday be kind and gentle husbands, loving and playful fathers, as well as proud and fiercely patriotic. Our little girl would be, in Doug's words, "Just like her mommy, with big blue eyes, and just a touch of tomboy to defend herself from her big brothers – but always, daddy's little girl."

Saying goodbye at the Columbus Airport in May was soul-crushing. I promised myself I wouldn't cry, but it was a foolish promise, and one I wasn't able keep. One thing I can truthfully say, it never once occurred to me that Doug would not return home safe. Our letters were happy and full of love. The intimate moments we had shared and memorized were whispered of and yearned for and always included in the letters between us. But what we wanted most, and what we actually had, broke our hearts and I counted the days to our Hawaiian R&R – which was never to be.

agreed to take humorously, although Christ's tenderness towards wid-

On September 13, 1969, my world stopped. I was working as a secretary in the office of a manufacturing company a couple of streets from my parents' home. Mother called me at work. "Honey, come home. There are some people here from the Army who need to talk to you. It's about Doug."

I remember my mouth felt like it was full of cotton. I couldn't say anything. I dropped the phone and with my heart in my throat, I ran out of the building and up the street. I didn't stop running until four blocks later, when I got to the house I grew up in, the home where I had always felt so safe and loved.

Parked in front of the house and looking out of place, was a long black car with something white printed on the side. I raced by without reading it, up the front steps, across the porch and in the front door. Just inside, stood two uniformed men locked to attention, their hands behind their backs. Their hats were tucked under their arms. Faces somber, they looked me straight in the eye and what I saw there told me that they wished they were anywhere but standing in my foyer waiting to deliver such dreadful news. Daddy and Mama stood nearby. Daddy had his arm around Mama's waist and she was crying quietly.

No. No. No. Dear God, what do they want? No, wait! I don't want to know! If they'll just go away, it won't be true.

"Mrs. Kempf, we regret to inform you that your husband, Sp4 Douglas S. Kempf, was killed while performing his duty in Vietnam on September 5..."

I didn't hear the rest of what the poor man had to say. Daddy said I fainted where I stood, just inside the front door in the foyer. When I came around, I was lying on the couch in my parents' living room – and then I remembered. Oh my God, I remembered, and I wanted to die, too. I was devoid of all feeling, except emptiness and grief. *Why? Why?*

Nothing would ever be the same. How could the world still seem so normal? The sun still shone through the curtains at the front windows. The birds still sang outside. I could hear a neighbor somewhere on our street mowing his lawn. How could that be? Didn't they know everything had changed? Only a few minutes before, those things had all been real. All of it clashed with my new reality and I suddenly felt I was losing my mind.

Then I focused hard, until only the couch was real. I was lying on the couch where Doug and I first held hands and hugged; the couch where we had our first disagreement, then kissed and made up. It was the same couch where I often sat in front of him on the floor between his knees, leaning back against him while we watched TV and he ran his fingers through my hair. It was the very same couch where he asked me to be his wife.

Bierce ~§~ *"Continuous persecution of widows and orphans is a crime.*

No, nothing could or would ever be normal again. My life was changed forever and I felt so completely alone, even though I was surrounded by people who cared and who also grieved like I did.

All I could do was cry, and I remember fighting a building anger. God, how could you do this...why would you reach down inside me and rip out my heart? There was so much grief and hurt and I went through the following weeks and months and even years in a fog. There are some things about that time that I can't remember at all, but oddly, there's one thing I will never forget. That was the first and only time I ever saw my father cry.

That day in 1969 was the worst day of my life, but it's carried me through some really bad times, too. There have been things that have happened since then, when I've said, "Yeah, this really hurts. It hurts like bloody hell, but I will survive, because I can tell you something about what real hurt is." For the rest of your life, something like this becomes your yardstick for measuring heartache. You know with a final certainty that nothing else can, or will, ever hurt you quite that badly again.

When I look up into the night sky, I pray that it isn't stars that I see, but actually little openings in Heaven's floor where the love of my lost one pours through and shines down to let me know he's happy.

A Day Like This

Patricia L. Goodman

On a day like this it rains so hard
that my deck is washed almost clean.
All I need is a scrub brush
to remove the rest of the bird mess.
Days like this should be cozy —
the storm keeping everyone inside —
if only he were in the next room
reading at his desk, waiting
for dinner.
On a day like this I find
a dead goldfinch on the deck,
weep as I bury it in the soggy garden,
worry that sometimes
I wish I were dead, too —
beside him wherever he is.
On a day like this a bright
pair of cardinals
forage for seed beneath the feeders,
share beak-to-beak
the goodness they discover.

How I Learned to Live on My Own
Jane Willingham

Despite two years of cancer treatments, Charlie's sudden stunning episode of headaches in March 2001 led to another series of treatments, this time for multiple brain cancers. Eventually his oncologist just dumped him into home hospice care saying, "There is nothing more I can do." Now it was late May, and Charlie and I had just had a very rough night with fitful sleep. As we drank our breakfast coffee he looked straight at me, so searchingly, and muttered, "I think I may be dying. What do you think?" After a long, long pause I stared at him and very quietly and simply said, "You may be right." There was another long silence. "I was hoping you wouldn't say that." Then another long pause while I searched for words and finally said, "Charlie, I've never lied to you." He just nodded.

When I buried his ashes in August, 2001 with a copy of Anne Bradstreet's "To My Dear and Loving Husband" on top, I didn't shed one tear. But afterwards, when I walked into our bedroom, I began to scream so loudly it rattled the blinds and scared my dog senseless. She crawled under the bed and wouldn't come out, and I wanted to join her. But I knew life must go on despite my pain, and so it did.

In the days to come, as I struggled to make a new life I realized suddenly that although I had never lied to Charlie, I had been lying to myself, expecting other people to help me pull out of my sadness. I was anxious to get back into plays and concerts, but when I asked friends to go with me they said, "I don't do things at night anymore. I don't feel safe." Although we were the same age, I realized they were just too set in their ways. I could see that if I really meant to start over, I must go it alone.

So I went by myself to concerts, going early to find a close parking place and packing a book in my purse. After I realized that once a play or a concert started I was alone with the people on the stage anyway, I quit worrying about being alone.

I just smiled in a friendly way to those seated around me, chatted if they seemed so inclined, and made a fast exit as soon as cast bows began. That was my first step in being a survivor.

I started volunteering. Since sitting alone in our usual pew only reminded me of what I had lost, I joined our church choir, used my piano skills to play for congregational singing once a month, and volunteered to teach a Bible study class for young couples.

They made me feel peppy, young, and useful when they laughed at my funny stories of child-rearing debacles. Next I began a singing group at

wine the very cup that was burned in the potter's oven?" Kahlil Gibran

the Senior Center made up of fragile members who had begun to lose it, but could still find pleasure singing familiar old songs. The center needed an official song, so I wrote one: "We Love the Center, Our Home Away from Home." And the center really became a second home for me as I took classes in watercolor, Italian, memoir writing, aerobics, and even tap dancing, – a colossal mistake. (I now realize I was only doing it so my grandchildren could brag that "My GrandJane takes tap dancing.")

Now that I am alone, I search the newspaper for fun things that are free. A local hardware store has "Ladies Nights" that teach me how to fix busted toilets, and do simple repairs on electrical things. I go to every art reception and student event at high schools and colleges. Many of these offer refreshments, too!

And speaking of food, I eat real meals, not fast food stuff. Standing at my kitchen counter and eating is a no-no at my house. Once a week I cook something big like a chicken pie or a meat loaf so I can invite guests to eat with me. Having neighbors over for meals helps us to know each other better and I can have confidence that they will help me out in emergencies just as I help them. Recently when a neighbor's well pump broke down, I never hesitated to let them run a hose to my house until their pump was fixed. Knowing their pets helps, too. My dog's best friend, Scooter, stays with me when

~§~ *"You can clutch the past so tightly to your chest that it leaves*

Carol has a business trip, and in turn she looks after Lulu when I need help.

Being physically active helps me survive happily. Every morning I begin my day sitting outside in my hot tub. Even when snow is on the ground I trudge out in my boots to sit there quietly, stare up at the trees, watch the sun rise, inhale the early air, listen to the birds, do five hundred stretches, and plan my day. Although I walk Lulu daily, my best walks are alone, making the two mile round trip from my house to the main road.

As I walk I reflect, quote poetry, and sing. If the weather is too bad for outdoor walking I hit the malls for a one hour fast nonstop walk and do it early before the stores open.

Since I live on Social Security and a small annuity, money is short at my house. I love to enter contests and continually fill out entry blanks hoping to win something. For me, such optimism is invigorating, and once I actually did win – a ten-day, all-expense trip to Italy, just for filling out a Ragú Spaghetti Sauce entry blank! You can see that I'm a dreamer, and I save up to make some of my dreams come true. Two years ago I went to Oxford, England, to study the Tudors for a month. It was expensive, but fulfilled a life-long dream. I saved for two years for that trip, went by myself, not with a group, and enjoyed it immensely.

My last piece of advice is to keep smiling. Smile constantly, even when you don't feel like smiling and it will get to be a habit that others will notice. Never discuss your ailments or personal problems, but *do* join in enthusiastically when neighbors are griping about local or national issues. I guarantee *that* will make you feel better. For more than eleven years I have been alone in my house. It is tough to come to terms with loneliness. Fifty good years of being friends and buddies as well as great sex partners is not easily replaceable. I admit that. But I have learned to put those special memories on a shelf and only take them down now and then. I let my past life be a platform of happiness that I can stand on to look ahead into a future of more happiness.

Little Knives

Frieda W. Landau

The cap **on** the toothpaste, no towels on the floor
No tripping over the shoes in the hall
No wisecrack at a silly sitcom
The vegetable you'll never buy again
The fresh-baked pie too big for just one
The hollow echo of unshared laughter
All the little things that catch you unaware
And shred the tattered remnants of your heart

Life, After

Marian Kaplun Shapiro

The morning's spent
buying toilet paper, Kleenex, and toothpaste
at the CVS. You should get a newspaper,
you think. Keep up. You buy less now than
you used to. You swipe your MasterCard and sign
with the un-pen, hit enter. The terminal
beeps, blinks, and thanks you. The clerk says,
Have a nice day, looking elsewhere. *You
too,* you say, already out the door. Couple
of blocks. Home. Unpack. *That's my exercise,*
you practice joking when you see someone to joke
with. Maybe Dr. Whatshisname, next week.
You read your *Times,* sort-of, now that there's no
    one
to argue with. Or kiss. Headlines go in
and out of focus. Water boarding. Wall Street.
Hurricane. Medicare.

Afternoon.
There's lunch, of course. Not very hungry.
Not hungry at all, when you come down to it,
but one has to eat, doesn't one? Another

~§~ *"The pain passes, but the beauty remains." Pierre Auguste Renoir*

bowl of cereal? Why not. Then a walk?
Too hot/cold/rainy/snowy/sunny
(bad for the skin) to bother. Make some tea.
Open the mail. Pay the cable bill. Clip
a coupon from the supermarket flyer. Sleep.
A nap takes care of one or two dead hours. Better
than the prefab noise of sitcom laughtracks, and
of gameshow contestants jumping up and down
and shrieking when they win, the losers, good sports
all, grinning their most sincere congratulations,
gripping their deluxe BluRay player instead
of the keys to a red Farrari.

And evening. That's
the best of all, because the day is almost over.
It's dark out now; *not safe for you to drive,*
you might be getting cataracts you'll say, in case
a friend should call, having an extra ticket to
the symphony. Soon it will be time to put
on your pajamas. Meanwhile there's the early
news to keep you company at dinner, which
is the leftover from a dinner from
some yesterday or other. Afterwards you can
reward yourself with TV reruns, one of which
reminds you of the time when you... Another life,
you say, shutting it off. Your children grow
     impatient.
They want to know why you don't answer all their
     emails
and their voice messages. I'm so busy,
you say. You don't understand. I have to work.

~§~ *"Grief is itself a medicine."* William Cowper ~§~ *"Parting is all we*

Letter Sent Up a Kite String

Joan Peronto

It's been five years
of driveway ice
CPA's
plumbers
mechanics
crabgrass-tansy-dandelions
children wandering
in and out of marriage
and employment
chipmunks in the walls
wasps in the attic
swifts in the chimney.
How about a trade?
You get down here
and fix your kids
I'll come up there
sit on a cloud
and watch.

Remembering Summer Evenings
Alice King Greenwood

Picture two white wicker chairs placed close together on the patio, armrests barely touching. That was, by far, the nicest place to sit outside in early evening. The waning sun made silhouettes of trees and sent its last rays peeking through fence slots, painting the grass with alternating stripes of green and gold.

"Come sit a while," you said, smiling, and pulled me down into my chair, so close to yours our hands just touched. Then interlocked.

Our eyes followed the stepping stones, past the garden filled with fragrant roses, to the edge of the lawn until we reached the little pond. Its splashing waterfall invited us to listen to its song. Fat green frogs joined in with their raspy croaks, softened by the drone of dragonflies. A family of baby turtles, following their mother, rustled their way through tall iris leaves, looking for a good place to spend the night.

Over the fence leaped the neighbor's big yellow cat. He crept silently to the pond and sat motionless for long minutes on his haunches, half-hidden in thick honeysuckle vines. He eyed the unsuspecting koi in the pond, hoping they would swim by close enough for him to pounce upon or snatch with his paw. But having no success in that venture and tiring of the game at last, he slowly stretched his legs, and wandered home.

A shimmering hummingbird zoomed to the feeder to suck his last savory swig of the day. Fascinated, we watched as he reveled in the sugary water until his thirst was quenched. For a while he hovered near our heads, chit-chitting as if to thank us for the drink, before whizzing off into the twilight.

A convention of raucous sparrows gathered in the sycamores and sweet-gums for their final session of the day. They twittered their personal messages from one tree to the next, like the Walton family's nightly ritual, until all had said "Goodnight." Then the sun clicked off, and night settled in.

Tonight on the patio, intense darkness envelops your empty wicker chair, envelops my untouched hand. "Come sit a while," I whisper.

All is silent. But like the fragrance of the rose garden, the times we shared still linger in the shadows on summer evenings.

total detachment, which excludes the ability to experience happiness."

Tense Dating

Cathy Bryant

When my husband was dying, he made me promise to find love again, as I was only in my fifties. I hated making the promise but he insisted, saying that a loving nature should never be wasted. It was a wonderful final gift to me, as it meant that I felt much less guilt than my other widowed friends when I found myself ready to think about a relationship again, many years later.

There was only one problem – no matter how well I got on with a man, no matter how we clicked or sparked or had a multitude of things in common, I was never asked out on a date. It was a bit of a mystery to me, and knocked my confidence badly.

"Men seem to like me, but they don't want to date me," I explained sadly to my (also widowed) friend, Anne.

"Well, I can't see why," she said, which was kind of her. And it was thanks to her that I found out what was wrong.

It was at a lovely evening dinner dance, at which a charming man had danced with me. When we finished the dance he came over and chatted to me where I sat with Anne – and then excused himself politely and melted into the night.

"See?" I said to Anne. "No one wants to go out with me."

"Oh my dear, dear friend," she said to my surprise, her eyes starring with tears. "They do want to go out with you! You chat away with them, so friendly, and then they ask, 'Are you married?' – and you reply, 'Yes, very happily, for twenty-four years.' And then you carry on talking! That's why they go off – they're disappointed. I bet that's happened loads of times!"

She was right. I said it automatically, without thinking at all. Of course I was married!

I had a bit of a cry with Anne, and then we did some practicing, with Anne asking me, *Are you married?* and my replying, *I WAS married, very happily, for twenty-four years.*

And like most widowhood experiences it involved tears and laughter, and a small step forward with the help of a friend.

Extraordinary Time

Molly Seale

I live in extraordinary time. But for much of my life, even though it was a full and rich life, I lived in ordinary time.

What changed *my* time from ordinary to extra-ordinary occurred at 6:30 a.m. on June 7, 1997. My husband had awakened earlier and dressed for his daily five-mile run. It was a Saturday, and I was sleeping in. The leap into extra-ordinary time, for me, began with a crash. I thought it was a cat, knocking over a lamp. But when I looked around, I saw nothing. I turned over to return to sleep, and then I heard my middle child cry, "Daddy, Daddy, what's wrong? Daddy! What's wrong?" I leapt from bed. Bob lay in the hallway, outside of our bedroom, lost in a grand mal seizure. I called 911 and two hours later, standing in the emergency room of the local hospital, I was informed by the attending ER physician that my husband had a tumor in his brain.

From the moment of that crash, my life ceased to be ordinary. My *time* ceased to be ordinary. Indeed, all − every last precious moment − was extra-ordinary.

Bob suffered from a glioblastoma multiforme, a grade IV astrocytoma – a tumor with the potential to double its size in ten days. In less than five days, we were told he had between eight and twelve months to live, that there was no cure, that the best treatment that could be offered was six weeks of full head radiation.

One day, a few months after he'd become ill, I went for a walk. I dreaded coming home to the sadness of our extraordinary time, to the knowledge that soon our lives would change even more, that he would be taken from us.

As I rounded the corner to our house, I saw Bob sitting on our front porch. When he saw me, he waved. My heart lurched. I swallowed hard. By the time I reached him, I was in tears. Although his head had been shaved for his first surgery, the radiation had eradicated whatever hair might have grown back, and his scalp had been scorched and shriveled by it. His swollen face already showed the effects of massive dosages of Decadron, taken to reduce brain swelling. His gait was altered. In a matter of months, he had aged about twenty-five years.

And yet, he was Bob.

As I climbed the steps to the porch, now crying, I sat beside him.

"What's wrong?" he asked.

I looked at him, amazed that he would ask such a question. Not able to answer, I cried more.

He pulled me onto his lap, "Molly, I'm alive. And I will live...until I die."

He looked at me kindly and sympathetically, as if he knew something I didn't know.

And then I understood. My tears evaporated.

He would live until he died, as would I, as would we all.

I wish I could say that the remainder of his life was so calm, assured, courageous, and wise. But of course it wasn't. He was human. He didn't want to die. He wanted to live. He didn't want to leave us – his wife, his three children. He wanted to *stay*.

But his words reverberated in my mind and heart throughout the duration of his illness. And after. And to this day. "I will *live*, until I die." No longer was time, was life, ordinary. Only extraordinary. Sixteen months, five brain surgeries, and three experimental surgeries after his diagnosis, Bob died at home, surrounded by the loving presence of many – friends, family, and even strangers who came to lend a hand. Angels, I believe. Companions in the extraordinary.

The Year of Firsts

James Escher

Shirley endured her year of firsts without him.
First Thanksgiving, first Christmas,
first New Year's (his favorite
with cabbage for luck and all that).
First Valentine's was sad; he was such
a romantic. And just when she thought
she'd given up on happiness, the first spring came
with first robins, then first summer
followed. Wasn't that a hummingbird?
First grandbaby is due in December.
And tonight, her first date, well, just dinner really,
but she's as nervous as she was for her first prom.

Move!

Carole Creekmore

The rushing water endlessly swirls, slaps, and crashes against the jagged rocks in the twisting mountain river. Balancing on a rock hanging out over the maelstrom, I wonder one more time what in the world I am doing, hesitate a moment – and then jump into the chaos of wild water and rocks. Swimming quickly around the rocks and through the thrashing water to the riverbank, I rejoin the others in my raft guide class waiting on the shore.

This professional raft guide class was a surprise gift arranged by my husband Chuck, just before he died unexpectedly. Grieving and left with the dilemma of returning his gift so far from my usual nature or using it, I decided to take a chance and attend. I had nothing else to lose. As a result, I learned that I guided rafts well and made rafting a safe and enjoyable adventure for my passengers. Suddenly alone, I am glad that I found the confidence and belief in myself to try whitewater raft guiding in my fifties.

All my life before Chuck, I had been careful and studied in my decisions, much more of a logical thinker and bookworm than a risk-taker. The years

grief like the grief that does not speak." *Henry Wadsworth Longfellow* married to Chuck gave me a greater curiosity about adventure, travel, and testing the waters, so to speak. I was intrigued by then-alien possibilities and supported by his encouragement. Now, I find myself alone, but gladly facing rather than turning away from new challenges and possible adventures.

Going from timid to willing – maybe even occasionally daring – I have learned to direct my life and my choices. I enjoy the feelings of satisfaction from these attempts, successful or not. Inspired to select my own path and life journey, I have found the confidence to move forward to meet other challenges rather than just retreating into my old, safe habits. I finally realize the importance of knowing where I want my life to go, no matter what the challenge.

In the years since Chuck died, I have continued to choose my paths with more and more confidence. My goals are to swim, not float through life, to learn about myself and the world around me. Adjusting to adventures alone, whether traveling down a whitewater river or across an ocean on a cruise, I have realized that I actually like myself and my own company. I now enjoy the balance of new people, places, and even adventures in my life.

What started as a grief-coping decision to attend raft guide school ended as one of my personal victories. Step by step, I have regained a certain confidence in myself, an assurance that my family and friends see in me as well. My life now has become a personal journey of new dimensions.

~§~ *"Every one can master a grief but he that has it."* William Shake-

Holding On

Linda O'Connell

On the nightstand: his watch,
a ring from his water glass,
retirement pin on the dresser,
a treasure from his past.

His slippers by the bedside,
on the door knob, his shirts,
eye glasses on the bureau;
my lonely heart hurts.

I slip my fingers into his gloves
feel the size of his hand,
hold tight to the memories
of a wonderful man.

After Your Husband Dies

Marissa McNamara

Learn to take care of the hurt places.
   Learn to love your God,
   whoever she is,
   your mouth around the sacred *om*,
   the throat pushing out another *amen*.

Learn your lonely heart, unmasked and bare.
   Know that sadness passes
   and that it returns, that it passes again,
   that it lives now in you,
   a part of your flesh that opens and closes,
   a part of your flesh now like wings
   unfurled then tucked tight
   to your fragile body.

Learn to feel the heat between your palms,
   the stretch in your neck
   as it bends in humility, and do what you do —
   turn the key in the lock, steep tea,
   read and watch TV and go out and run
   and sit – yes – sit and throw yourself down
   and cry without shame
   let the sobs come up from your belly,

your heart, your lungs,
let the body shudder and wring itself out.

Do this more than once. Do it until you are limp
and let people touch you and enfold you
and let them hold some of your sorrow,
for they want to.

Learn to miss him. Yes, miss him until the missing
becomes a taste on your tongue
a stone in your palm
a piece of you, because it is,
but even bullets lodged in the flesh
can be accepted by the body.

And when it has been a year or two
or five or ten, write a poem
reminding yourself how to love.
Let the words spill from your fingers
like the tears that come more slowly now.

Write not to make him come alive
but to tell the world that you are alive
even though for the rest of your life
you will live after he has died.

The Condolence Call

Gretchen Fletcher

"She was too busy feeling grief to dress like grief."
Zora Neale Hurston

Wearing widow's weeds of fuchsia,
as shocking as untimely death,
the raw color of the new wound
hidden in the breast
under that brave blouse
he liked on her,

she ushers us graciously into the hush
of their room he'll not come back to,
past clusters of family members
and the table loaded with food
from friends who didn't know
what else to say.

She waves her hands
through the empty air
illustrating the stories of their life
together with gestures. As if calling
him back, they flutter as if seeking
to hold his again.

She has rejected black
and opted for bright instead.
The room glows with her fuchsia
and his so very recent presence.
The food lies uneaten,
the tears, as yet, unshed.

Night

Frieda W. Laudau

I go to bed late, later than I should
Finding reasons to stay awake
Watching old movies in black and white
And playing endless solitaire
Or calling unseen friends overseas
Where the new day is almost half done
But friends, however dear, have their own lives
At last, in the grey light before dawn
When sleep overcomes all excuses
I face the desolation of an
Empty bed the rising sun cannot warm

Morning Ritual

Helen Padway

I hug you every morning
by hanging my jacket
over your abandoned brown tweed,
on my door hook.

This is not automatic. I am aware,
careful and deliberate despite
the futility of my gesture. Some days,

the hanger swings a little
as though in greeting – some days
it does not move. My coat sleeves

still warm surround your empty ones.
The silk lining caresses the woolen fabric.
One day your son will remember

where this sport coat hangs
and claim it for his own —
taking from me my mourning comfort.

Stepping Out

Wayne Scheer

Elizabeth had finally accepted widowhood with grace and humor. She even changed the recording on her answering machine to say: "As unlikely as it may seem, the widow Grayson is not home at present."

The last thing she expected, nearing her seventy-sixth birthday, was the message that greeted her when she returned home from the grocery store.

"Hello Elizabeth, or should I say Widow Grayson? I love your message. This is Jack Kearns, a friend of Mary and Bill Lindsay. We met last week at the art auction in Atlanta. Heaven help us, but Mary has taken it into her head to fix us up. Well, to be honest, it wasn't entirely her idea. I asked about you with, perhaps, too much fervor. Anyway, she's concocting a plan to invite you for dinner while neglecting to say I would be there. But I've decided at our age there's no time for games. Would you like to meet for breakfast? I'll leave my phone number. If I don't hear from you, I'll try again tomorrow evening."

Elizabeth shook her head. Good grief, she was being asked out. When the shock wore off, she played the message again. This time, she enjoyed Jack's honesty. Like Leonard, her late husband, he sounded intelligent and honest, with an accent, like hers, that gave away his Southern roots.

She put away the few items she had purchased and recalled meeting Jack at the auction. She was there to buy a painting by a local artist she admired and couldn't be bothered with small talk. Still, she remembered Jack as tall and thin, with longish white hair. She thought he looked like a man who smoked a pipe, although thank goodness he didn't smell of tobacco. She also recalled that they had exchanged a few words about art, and he appeared knowledgeable and unpretentious.

For the first time since her husband's death three years earlier, she found herself thinking of another man. Should she feel guilty or amused, she wondered.

She considered what the children would think. Barbara would probably say it's about time. Bryan, more like his father, would make a joke and shrug it off. The grandchildren's reactions would undoubtedly be dismay that an old lady might have a gentleman interested in her.

She wanted to call Janice, her friend since high school, but Janice's cancer had recently spread to

over your head, but you can prevent them from building nests in your her liver. She would be in no mood to gossip about a man asking her out. Waving her hand in the air, she tried putting the idea out of her mind.

She turned on Vivaldi's "Concerto in G Minor," but her mind wandered to Jack. She recalled how he had focused on her when they spoke, as if he were truly listening to what she said. She regretted being preoccupied with the auction.

What foolishness! After spending more than fifty years with one man, how could she even entertain such thoughts? She had finally grown comfortable with her new life. Why would she want to risk...

Risk what? Eating dinner by herself? Dashing off to the grocery story for a couple of items as an excuse to get out of the house? Her comfort was little more than resignation; she knew that. She had never been one to passively accept what could be changed for the better. Why was she so accepting now?

It would be wonderful, almost regenerative, listening to music or enjoying good food with a thoughtful man. She never felt at ease with couples like the Lindsays, always imagining herself a third wheel. And, although she had a few women friends, she enjoyed the company of men.

She had grown accustomed to being the only woman in the boardroom as a fundraiser for non-profits. She learned to enjoy intelligent men and avoid the bores. Most of all, she could come home and laugh with Leonard about her adventures in the so-called man's world of corporate finance. Leonard understood little of what she did, and she understood even less about cardio-pulmonary research, but they appreciated each other's intelligence. And they laughed. She tried recalling the last time she had laughed freely at a clever remark, instead of forcing a smile at an insipid, poorly told joke.

What harm could there be in sharing coffee and conversation with an interesting man?

She turned towards the telephone, remembering he said he'd call back tomorrow evening. Would it be forward of her to phone him? Should she at least wait a bit longer? The thought made her smile. She imagined her mother, representing at least seven generations of Southern women, frowning at the notion of her calling a man.

Leonard had often observed that a man never outgrew his adolescent insecurities. Apparently, the same held true for a woman, no matter her age.

Pushing herself out of her chair, she replayed the message, this time copying Jack's number and calling it, not allowing herself time to think.

The telephone conversation went well. Once she identified herself, Jack sounded relieved. He said he hated message machines and feared he had rambled like a dolt. Once they both admitted their awkwardness, they spoke comfortably.

Jack had been widowed for nearly five years and had suffered depression, but only recently realized it. He had spent so much energy assuring his children he was doing fine, he ignored his own feelings. To his surprise, over cocktails, he had admitted to Mary and Bill that he wanted to date again. That's when Mary told him about Elizabeth and arranged their introduction at the auction.

"You mean it wasn't a chance meeting?"

"There are no coincidences in Mary's world." They laughed.

After a pause, he added, "Mary describes you as brilliant, witty and kind. A virtual saint."

"The operative word is 'virtual,'" she had assured him. "I'll have to catch up on my reading of both the Gospels and Oscar Wilde." She felt proud of her little witticism and relieved he seemed to get it.

With that, they arranged to meet for lunch the next day, both admitting that neither wanted to wake up early enough for a breakfast date.

After she hung up, Elizabeth tried recalling which of them had used the word "date."

That evening, memories of her first date with Leonard haunted her. They were both in college – he a junior, majoring in biology, and she a sophomore English major. They had attended a school production of *King Lear*. She was surprised a science major knew so much about theater.

Despite her own naïveté, he hung on to her every word. Leonard had a way of listening with his whole self, much like Jack. When she spoke, he'd lean in towards her, his hand on his chin. His eyes focused on her, as if she were the only person in the room. She had known immediately Leonard was special.

Even after he went on to medical school and she earned an MBA, they remained friends. When Leonard finally asked her to marry him, her mother replied, "It's about time."

So how, after a lifetime of living with and loving her best friend, could she be thinking of another man?

She ate her dinner alone, grilled chicken breast with beets and a salad with a pear vinaigrette dressing she had prepared yesterday from a new recipe. Too acidic, she thought. It needed sweetening.

She read for a while and watched some television before deciding to go to bed early. Her mind wandered to the first time she and Leonard were intimate. She could still feel the comfort of his arms, the way she relaxed and let go of her inhibitions. It would be good to rest her head on a man's chest, to smell a man's muskiness.

That night she dreamed of Jack. Was it a sex dream? Certainly not. She couldn't imagine Jack that way. Or herself. Although the details dissolved with the morning light, she felt aroused and distraught.

In the shower, she made up her mind to call off the lunch date. She'd tell him the truth: she wasn't

"Mourning is one of the most profound human experiences that it is

ready. She imagined him joking, "You're not ready to eat lunch? How about dinner then?"

She knew how foolish she sounded. How often had she advised her own children to step out of their comfort zones, to take chances. When her daughter doubted her ability to succeed in law school, Elizabeth responded, "How will you know if you don't try?" Barbara, who had recently made full partner at her firm, told her numerous times how important those words were to her. If only she could follow her own advice.

Now a new fear taunted her as she stepped out of the shower and considered her reflection in the mirror. Her body looked like she had stayed in a swimming pool too long. Recalling how proudly she had presented her young, firm body to Leonard, she pushed up her sagging beasts and watched them fall, not bounce.

After drying herself and putting on an oversized, comfortable robe, she poured a cup of coffee and finalized her decision. She would call Jack and cancel plans. No need to torture herself any longer.

When she reached for the phone, she saw a missed call on the message machine. She played it.

"Hello, Elizabeth. It's Jack. I hope it's not too early to call. If you're anything like me, you've had a restless night. Until a few minutes ago, I had decided to cancel our plans. I feared I wasn't ready to meet a woman I wanted to know better. I'm being a

possible to have... The deep capacity to weep for the loss of a loved one

perfect fool, I know – I assure you I'm not usually this indecisive. Would you please call me when you get a chance and assure me I'm not a total idiot? Perhaps between us we can strengthen our collective nerve."

Elizabeth smiled and, it seemed for the first time since yesterday, exhaled. She reached for her reading glasses and called Jack's number.

Job Interview

Angie Francis

Spring.
You'll need a new suit, she says.

The old suit
dark navy, dust
on the shoulders,
pockets frayed.
Bought for some
grandmother's
funeral.

It's twenty years old, for god's sake, she says

From the racks,
she gleans a charcoal 42

and to continue to treasure the memory of that loss is one of our no-

long, two ties – one
cherry red silk – one
checkerboards, blue and gray.
Two shirts – one white –
one robin's egg blue,
cordovan belt,
socks – gray.

He tumbles
to the fitting room. White
chalk slashes
charcoal cloth.

Summer.
Hurry with the clothes, they say.

She chooses the charcoal
gray once more, gray
suit, cherry red silk tie, shirt
bone white
and underwear,
gray socks, cordovan belt and wingtips

New suit
gone burial shroud.

Changing Direction

Aline Soules

Someone turns into my driveway,
their car headlights sweeping past
my neighbor's dogwood to face
my closed garage door.

I hear the crunch of wheels on gravel,
Then silence when the car stops.

It could have been you in your Jeep,
coming home to dinner, but
you've been dead two weeks
and my world is full of never.

The Jeep in the garage will soon
be sold and I am in the kitchen
eating dinner by myself.

The unknown someone backs out
headlights reversing across the lawn.

A simple wrong turn
easily corrected.

Parking Garage

Thelma Zirkelbach

This afternoon I have my annual check-up with Dr. S., my gastroenterologist. I head for the Texas Medical Center and drive up the ramp to the entrance of Parking Garage 2. Immediately my heart speeds up and I'm overcome by a familiar feeling of dread. I slow down and notice there is a new parking system. I don't understand the instructions at first and this adds a layer of confusion to my already jangled emotions. At last I figure out what to do and receive a yellow "smart chip," that I stash away for my eventual exit.

The gate opens and I drive farther up and into the dim garage. For me, this is not a parking area but a cavern of memories. Garage 2 is across from M.D. Anderson Cancer Center, where my husband Ralph spent the last seven months of his life. I parked here every day. The year of his battle with leukemia, I spent over $2000 on parking alone.

The garage is large and gloomy and exudes the faint smell of automobile exhaust. In winter a stiff breeze blows through it; in summer there's no breeze, just dense heat and humidity. It's always crowded here. I can't begin to estimate the time I spent the year of Ralph's hospitalization, driving from floor to floor, up and down the aisles, searching for an empty space. As I make the same drive today, I recognize spots where I once parked. I remember the trials of maneuvering into the narrow spaces in the middle aisle. Backing up, straightening, backing up again before I could inch into a spot without scraping the paint off the car next to me. Many times I could barely squeeze my 110 pound frame out of my vehicle's door.

When I left, usually around ten o'clock at night, the garage was eerily quiet. The only sound I heard was the robotic male voice from the machine where I paid for parking: "Please insert your parking ticket with the stripe facing up and to the right." I rarely encountered anyone, even a security guard, but I wasn't afraid. I was too focused on my husband's deteriorating condition, on the fear of losing him, and honestly, I was too tired to care if I ran into a mugger or some other unsavory character. I never expected to, anyway; people who park in cancer hospital garages have other things on their minds. Sometimes when I got to the car, I was so filled with despair that I would sit slumped in the seat, my cheek resting on the steering wheel, and let the tears come. Then I would pull myself together and drive home to an empty house.

I lost my car twice in the garage, once at night and once on a brutally hot afternoon two days before Ralph died. I wandered back and forth through the labyrinthine building from floor to floor. There were gray Toyotas everywhere, too many of them, but none of them seemed to be mine. Sweat soaked my clothes, my hair. My purse was too heavy; perspiration made my glasses slip down my nose. Tears mingled with the moisture on my cheeks. I had made an appointment with an estate attorney and I knew I would be late. I phoned my son as I trudged through the garage and he said, "Ask for a later appointment. Tell them you're waiting for the doctor. Don't say you've lost your car. They'll think you're a nut case."

"Okay." I followed my son's instructions, but I knew I was a nut case, confused, bewildered, a woman on the verge of losing the dearest part of her life.

Back on the first floor of the garage, I picked up the phone to parking services and asked for help locating my car. A nice grey-haired man appeared a few minutes later and drove me back through the garage. "Could the dealership maybe have repossessed your car?" he inquired politely.

"No, it's paid for." I'm not a debtor; I'm a nut case.

Finally we found my car. I thanked the man, drove out of the garage and got lost on the way to the attorney's office.

Loss permeated that year. Soon after Ralph's leukemia diagnosis, I lost my mother. She lived a few months past her hundredth birthday and then on a November afternoon she died. The last link to my childhood was gone.

One day a few months later, I parked and dropped my wallet next to my car. I noticed it was missing when I opened my purse in Ralph's hospital room. I was frantic, but when I rushed back to the garage, I found it untouched. I lost a lot of things while Ralph was sick: my keys, a folder from my office, my wallet again. I recovered every-thing...except him.

I parked in Garage 2 during Hurricane Rita. Houstonians left the city, crowding the highways, running out of gas. Afraid Ralph would take a turn for the worse and I wouldn't be able to reach him, I stayed at the hospital. Not surprisingly, the parking garage was full when I reached the Medical Center. What if I had to park on the roof? Goodbye, car. Fortunately, after driving up and down the rows for about twenty minutes, I found a space just down the last ramp from the roof. My suitcase, crammed with clothes, books, and important papers, had wheels; but I eat three meals a day no matter what the circumstances and I had a bag of food, which I had to lug to the elevator. My back hurt, a physical ache to add to my emotional pain. The hurricane turned out to be a non-event, but I kept an eye on the garage from Ralph's window throughout the next two days.

I remember the first time I parked here, seven years ago when Dr. S. moved from the University of

Texas Medical School to M.D. Anderson. Patients were welcome to follow him, and I did.

I felt squeamish the first time I parked in the garage and entered the enormous building that houses the cancer center. While I waited to be called into an examining room, a young man approached me and explained he was doing a survey for one of the hospital departments. Could he ask me a few questions? I nodded and he said, "Are you currently receiving chemotherapy?"

"Oh," I said. "I'm not a cancer patient." We were both embarrassed. He apologized profusely and moved on, leaving me to wonder if I should carry a warning sign, *I Do Not Have Cancer*, to prevent such uncomfortable encounters. By the next year I had forgotten. Cancer had struck, and I would accompany my husband through chemotherapy, a stem cell transplant, and numerous terrifying procedures and mishaps.

When I drove out of the garage the morning Ralph died, I suddenly wanted to turn around and head back in. The garage, though nothing more than a dank, unwelcoming area of concrete, was my final connection to him. It seemed more significant, more memorable than the hospital. But I was already past the exit; the automatic arm had dropped down behind me. Too late to turn back. I drove home.

Five years have gone by now since Ralph passed away. Five more visits to this building that

the rules. He leaves the party too soon, and leaves the other guests

symbolizes the ugliness and pain of Ralph's final year and the grief that followed. The cancer hospital has another garage, Garage 4. It's newer and airier with a sky bridge that connects it to the hospital proper. Why don't I park there, in a building untainted by memories? Because I am compelled to confront the demons of Garage 2, to remind myself I have survived and that whatever happens in the years to come, I am and will continue to be a survivor. And finally, I park here to prove to myself that I can.

Alone

Barbara B. Rollins

Custody of remote controls,
sovereignty over social calendar,
freedom from imposed pet peeves,
permitted to cook my favorite meals.
No one to see the mess I leave,
nobody to turn the volume down.
Who can I tell of the weirdness
of night after night here, alone?

Lingering at the Cemetery

June Rose Dowis

Seems like yesterday
we talked of weather…
supposed to rain

and that kiss
if you can call it that
more a peck on the cheek

did I sigh when you told me
you had forgotten the
dry cleaning…again

trivial moments take
on monumental meaning
in hindsight

the world just keeps
on revolving…
unaware

my last words
were not what
I'd have chosen

Had I known you
would take them
with you…forever

in a world so full and busy the loss of one creature makes a void so wide

Driver's Seat

Carol Faulkner Peck

You always were the driver
At times we shared the ride,
And I felt full, protected,
Sitting by your side.

But then our world collapsed on us,
Stole your strength and pride;
You became the passenger...
And took it in your stride.

All through the toxic treatments,
You still directed me;
I felt empty, helpless,
But kept you close to me.

Today I fetched your ashes
And placed that heavy urn
Into your soft, reclining chair...
The point of no return.

No longer am I traveling
Exhausted to the bone;
But now I'm in the driver's seat...
And traveling alone.

and deep that nothing but the width and depth of eternity can fill it

The Suit

Elaine L. Galit

It's the quiet ones who surprise you the most.

My husband Ray loved to just listen. At any party or family gathering someone would always ask, "Why so quiet?" His reply usually came as a smile. If he had something he wanted to express, he'd play his beloved piano. In later years, computer games held his attention. He was a rock; I was, and still am, the flittering bird, albeit an eagle. Our married life coasted along with the usual swirls and smooth waters. Until we'd been married some forty years.

Then he changed.

My calm, cool, and collected mate became a cranky tiger. A complete flip from positive to negative seemingly overnight. I'd always admired his calm demeanor when errant drivers cut him off or blew their horns unnecessarily. No more. Now he cursed them. He loved playing his computer games saying they gave him a sense of accomplishment when he beat the villain. Now he became the villain, yelling continually at the computer screen as though it had somehow cheated him. The quick hugs when I came into the room were no longer.

He was proud of the weight he'd lost. I realized something was wrong, but never guessed the reason.

Three years later I discovered why he'd changed. I think when he finally died of renal cancer after lingering in a hospital for months, his death surprised no one.

Except me.

I had spent the months in abject denial along with him until his mind snapped and he failed even to recognize me. After his death came the anger, then I wallowed in guilt. What had I done or not done and what could I have done better? My son finally helped me to understand that hindsight is foolish. Life must continue for the rest of us.

For many years the horror of his last days haunted me. No matter how hard I tried, that pain was what I remembered of the man with whom I'd spent forty-three years.

Until the day a stray thought obliterated the horror of his end of life. I was feeding Juni, our calico cat, when I remembered a morning when I'd left the shower to go into the master bedroom to dress. I stopped in the doorway in shock. A man was in the room with Ray!

Although I couldn't see him, I distinctly heard Ray say, "I don't understand. Why do you always wear the same suit every day? Don't you get tired of grey stripes?"

strength which will always spring up if thou will always look there."

I ducked behind the bathroom door and yelled. "Ray, who in the heck are you talking to? Who's here?"

Silence...then he burst out laughing.

"It's not funny," I hollered.

"Come out and see," he said between bouts of laughter.

I wrapped a towel around me and with caution stepped into the bedroom. With that, I joined in the laughter because there, in the corner of the room, was Tiger, our grey striped cat.

So I've struggled through the bouts of self-pity, the torrent of tears and the torn feelings of loss and focused on the smile of humor.

It was remembering this story that made me recall the Ray I'd always loved. I'd forgotten his best and most important trait; his sense of humor.

Thoughts of Ray's bizarre and clever sense of humor took over and I remembered his many funny jokes. How he made my children laugh each Thanksgiving when he'd do his turkey impression. How he loved to imitate Victor Borge on the piano, sliding off the bench onto the floor as he ended playing a piece. How he'd take the punch line of his favorite joke of the moment and repeat it many times making it fit into whatever the topic of conversation might be at the time. That day I felt reborn as his sense of humor poked holes in my grief.

As widows we take what we choose from the miasma of aversion that was a loved one's end of days. I choose to remember the "cat with the grey striped suit." I choose to remember life. I choose to remember humor.

Today, instead of those last days, I recall the good times, the fun times, the times of love requited.

Don't Tell Me to Have a Nice Day
Charlotte Wolf

Don't tell me, *Things will get better*
I don't want to hear, *Just take it one day at a time*
This day is bad enough, I don't want to think
    about this one
Why would I want to think about there being more
Let alone have to think about tomorrow.

Don't even try comforting me with that tired old
You have all those wonderful memories
You only remind me I have no future.

The five stages of grief? Simple
They are grief, grief, grief, grief and grief
They are missing and longing and *how do you*
    open the hood on this @#$%^&! car?
They are aching and crying and denying and
    being mad as hell
They are pacing an empty house at five o'clock

with gin in your hand
Talking to pictures on the walls.

They are the Chinese water torture of
*If only…What if?…Why him?…It should have
    been me…Why didn't I see this coming?*
Drip. Drip. Drip.

They are nightmare nights and unexpected
    mornings
They are cooking for one, but shopping for two
Dining with CNN, all you widows will get that
And that's another thing, do not call me *widow*, ever
I've been Mrs. John Wolf for fifty years, nothing's
    changed that.

Yeah, I'm into serious grief
Like watching two bent, white-haired people pick
    their way
Along the sidewalk hand in hand smiling at each
    other
*How dare they be a couple? What right? They
    must be in their nineties!*

Today, envy and bitterness are my hand-holding
    companions
So, don't tell me to have a nice day.

Garden, Remembered

Susanne Braham

Another spring of missing.
No outstretched hand
leading me through tulips
or past the buzzing bees,
those harbingers of bloom.

Assaulted, that fragrance
of hydrangeas!
While overhead the
cherry blossoms
danced on azure stage.
Transitory yellows —
swallowtails alighting —
sipping savory nectars,
flitting on.

You and I,
woozy with pollen,
drowning in our love hive.
And the bees, always the bees,
brutally obligatory.
They promised, menacing.

So too, our forays
through the lingering pink of petals
strewn upon the ground,
heightening desire.

Winter Through Widow Eyes
Linda A. Panczner

Fall concedes gracefully as snowflakes silently
   announce change.
She watches behind glass panes, safe from the
   elements
and from those who reach out to her.
Each flake dances downward unique and alone.
Only upon landing do they unite and gather
   strength.
Tumbling in precarious abandon, free yet fragile
without foundation until they merge below.
She sees herself through widow's eyes, above
   the rest,
hovering, unformed, unable to settle and connect.
Yet, she remains inside, not yet ready for a united
   front,
unwilling to dive into life's next phase.
Hiding in a winter hibernation.

we lose. Although we know that after such a loss the acute stage of

Apart

Aline Soules

I've given you away.
I don't know who got
your lungs or eyes or
bones, but your heart
went to a young woman
with two small children.
She wrote to say that it will
slowly give way to her body's
disease, but not before
she sees her children grow.

You're a busy man,
living in so many places
at the same time. Maybe
you breathe in the chest
of a man just down the street,
or look at a lake through the eyes
of a boy who has only known
its sound or the chill
of its lapping waves. Perhaps
you hike up a mountain
in the now-sturdy legs
of a woman on the other side
of the country.

mourning will subside, we also know that we shall remain inconsolable

Yet, the more those legs
take you away from me
and your heart pumps in another,
the more you breathe
to a different rhythm
and each of us sees people and places
the other will never know,
the more my empty heart
wonders if we have met again,
neither of us able to recognize
that we are together still.

Without You

Robyn Conley

I couldn't imagine not smiling at your grin
I couldn't imagine not aching when you hurt
I couldn't imagine not seeing you nibble your
    moustache
I couldn't imagine not hearing your laugh
I couldn't imagine not nodding off with you, each
    in our chairs
I couldn't imagine not hearing, "Love you, lady,"
I couldn't imagine not waking with you, stroking
    your hair

I still can't

and will never find a substitute. No matter what may fill the gap, even

the burly man

Meta E. Lee

motionless
my dog and i watched
the burly man

effortless
he heaved and tossed
bulging sacks into his van

twenty sacks of all those clothes
my husband wore
satin robe —
 shirts —
 shoes —
 slacks —
 and ahhh
so much more

t-t-thank you m'am
stammered the burly man
t-t-this will h-h-help others
t-t-that's for sure

the dog growled
i held his collar
the garage door creaked closed

if it be filled completely, it nevertheless remains something else." Sig-

motionless
the dog and i waited
the burly man drove away

we crouched upon the garage floor
his sweet head upon my knee
we sobbed and dozed
my dog and i

Memorial Bench

Peter D. Goodwin

I visited your bench today
your Memorial Bench
splashed your perfume —
sweet, pungent, sensuous —
over the weathered wood
its aroma mingling
with the wood of the bench
the wooded atmosphere of the park
the dampness of the day
dissolving into memory...

We often walked this path
past these very benches
rarely to stop and rest

mund Freud ~§~ "Give sorrow words; the grief that does not speak

rarely to note the memorial plaques
that I note so well today
along with yours...

I keep your ashes in an urn
on the top of a bookcase
which I ignore
as I go about the business
of living without you.
The green glaze
of that urn matches
the color of the knit dress
you wore when I first saw you
and what remains of you
is in that urn
sitting in lonely splendor
on the top of a bookcase
which I ignore
for those ashes are not you...

I don't know where you are
or if you are anywhere
perhaps a hummingbird
whose flash of red
sometimes pauses
and looks into
the dining room window
or that annoying woodpecker
that insistently taps
on my bedroom window
(challenging a reflection
a birder friend assures me)

knits up the o'er-wrought heart and bids it break." William Shake-

I only feel your presence
by this bench,
your bench…
where all the memories
come rushing back…

I have your perfume with me
I'll dab a little on the bench…
it's a French perfume
no longer available here
perhaps not even available
in France…
combining your sophistication
with your love for nature…
and wherever you are
if anywhere
here by this bench
we will be together…

Grief Morphing

Meta E. Lee

Grief invades her space
he barrels through the hollow rooms
he feints and charges
thumps his chest
with clenched fists he jabs
pummels the mourner to the floor

onrushing foul breath
he whoops out loud
hurtles around her
lurks and skulks

in the fullness of time
his somber melodies engulf her
as a plume of white vapor
he slithers to a window left ajar

smaller now
scarcely there
minces around on mouse feet
pirouetting he departs

his scent still lingers
heavy cloying
always there

fusion or despair, who can stay with us in an hour of grief and be-

Widowhood: Some Notes

Cathy Douglas

1. Nobody knows what to say to a person in grief, especially someone they don't know well. I used to wonder what to say too. I suggest "Condolences," or some related phrase, because it gives the person an easy reply: "Thank you." If you say "I'm sorry," it's awkward, because there's no obvious reply to it. You can't thank a person for feeling sorry, and a reply like "Me too" sounds flip. By offering condolences, you're making things easy on the grieving person, and helping the conversation move forward.

One time I said "I'm sorry" to a teenager who'd just lost his sister to leukemia, and he replied, "That's okay, it wasn't your fault."

2. Maybe this is stating the obvious, but widowhood means no more than the absence of marriage – that huge, all-encompassing life choice that most of us make when we're young and stupid. When a spouse dies, their absence is tangible. I've seen it compared to a missing limb, and there's a reason this has become a cliché: it's an apt comparison. But that isn't the thing that came to mind for me.

reavement, who can tolerate not knowing...not healing...not curing...

I used to have a cockatiel named Fred, who rode around on my shoulder. Fred didn't weigh really anything. But when he lifted off, after the initial push-off, it was as if his very absence was perched there in his place. The absence of a soul feels like that.

3. All the things that were ours are now mine. It's a scary, heady feeling. So many decisions and arrangements I have to make, and no sharer-of-life to discuss them with. This process occupies a huge amount of my time right now: talking to bankers, waiting on hold for insurance people, filling out government forms. Once this period of adjustment is over, I'll get back into ordinary life – work, family, volunteer work, writing. Except, everything will be different.

4. After my first son was born, I could never again doubt there were worlds beyond our own, because I saw their reflection in his newborn eyes. This was unexpected. Now, after being present for a death, I can never be afraid of it again. This, too, was wholly unexpected.

All of His Heroes

Terri Elders

It's not often I'm taken aback while simply waiting in line at the post office. This past week, though, I dropped in one morning to pick up stamps and glanced over at the glass display case spotlighting the new commemoratives. I stifled a gasp...and squelched a joyous yelp. Even my normally nonchalant late husband would have struggled to repress a squeal. I bet he'd have skittered right on over for a closer look.

Nearly a year has inched by since he died last spring, and as the anniversary of his death nears, I often start the day feeling sad. I find myself longing to share a bit of news. I'll wish I could recount how the neighbors across the way finally painted their house, how I can't get excited about the current batch of singers on *American Idol,* or how his favorite restaurant is staging a lobster fest. Right then I wished we could marvel together at these new stamps.

My gallant and gutsy husband had absorbed his diagnosis of pancreatic cancer with what seemed to me an almost heroic grace. He rarely com-

tears. *They are not the mark of weakness, but of power. They speak*

plained and never whimpered during those last months as he steadily declined.

"I can't tell you enough how brave I think you are," I'd said.

"Brave? Nah. Just accepting the inevitable," he answered. "Tom Mix wouldn't be boohooing. Neither would Wild Bill Elliott." He craned his neck to gaze at the lithograph on the wall above his favorite overstuffed chair.

The sepia-toned collage featured portraits of two dozen movie buckaroos, everybody from Johnny Mack Brown to John Wayne. Its caption, "All of My Hero's Are Cowboys," had made me grin when he first hung the picture when we moved into our retirement home.

"It's tough to make two mistakes in one word," I'd said, "but the artist managed. He's got a superfluous apostrophe and a misspelled plural. It should be h-e-r-o-e-s."

Ken laughed. "I'd never noticed before. I've had this for years, but I've always been too busy admiring those actors. I love Westerns because the good guys always win."

Ken claimed his mom had named him for one of the Western stars in the painting, Ken Maynard. "I'm just glad he was the one she idolized, rather than a couple of the other guys up there. I can't imagine having gone through life as Hoot or Hop-along."

more eloquently than ten thousand tongues. They are the messengers

I sidled over for a closer look. "Hmmm. There's also Lash Larue and Crash Corrigan. Lash or Crash would have been dashing."

"I'll settle for plain old Ken."

He bragged that he must have seen a hundred Westerns by the time he hit third grade. His mom dropped him off at the theater every Saturday afternoon and he'd watch double features. During the summers while she worked he'd usually go three or four times a week. He listened to *The Lone Ranger* and *The Cisco Kid* on the radio and later watched every Western series that appeared on television.

The only song he knew all of the words to was "Paladin," the theme tune from *Have Gun – Will Travel*, a late '50s TV show later adapted to radio. Whenever that show appeared on one of the many cable channels Ken subscribed to during his last years, he'd record each episode and watch them over and over.

"He's a true hero," Ken explained. "Many of the movie cowboys jump right into a fight, but Paladin first tried to settle disputes without violence whenever he possibly could. He not only had brains, he had class. He loved good food, good wine and sharp clothes."

Just like my husband, I thought, who served up even simple grilled burgers gorgeously garnished, routinely sniffed and swirled before sipping and insisted on ironing his own shirts to get the collars and cuffs just right.

"Here's the thing about Westerns," he'd told me, after watching an episode of *Cheyenne* just days before he died. "Life's uncertain enough just as it is. You don't need any extra ambiguity in your entertainment. So many of the new movies you watch leave too many questions unanswered for me. I want everything crystal clear at the end. I want to believe that justice always will out."

In Ken's case I like to think that it did. He tried to be a good guy until the very end. He died in discomfort, yes, but without experiencing the pain that so many with a similar diagnosis have had to endure. He chalked it up to karma.

Now as the post office line shortened, I had a clearer view of the display case. The new stamps, "Cowboys of the Silver Screen," bear portraits of four of the men in Ken's lithograph: William S. Hart, Tom Mix, Gene Autry and Roy Rogers. All four wear jaunty white cowboy hats. Though two smile and two scowl, anybody could tell they're all good guys.

Tears clouded my eyes, but my mouth twisted into a smile as I approached the counter. For the past year I've been sending birthday and Christmas cards to my husband's closest friends, some who date back to childhood, and to his three adult sons and their families. Now I'll have something special to affix to the envelopes that will be a happy reminder of Ken's lifelong passion.

"I'll take five sheets of the cowboy stamps," I said, reaching into my purse for a tissue. I wiped a tear from my cheek.

The post office worker opened her drawer and counted out several sheets. "Got a spring allergy?" she asked, as I sniffed.

"No. I'm just absolutely overjoyed by these stamps."

"Well, they are bright and cheery," she said, totaling my tab.

"They remind me so much of my husband."

"Whatever," she said, shrugging and reaching for my credit card. While she swiped it, she glanced from the stamps to my face and back, and then shook her head.

I ducked my head to hide a smirk. She thinks I'm the odd one, I thought. I bet she doesn't even know that Paladin's horse was named Tanglefoot or that Tom Mix's was Tony! I bet she thinks that Cheyenne is just a city in Wyoming!

I headed for home much more lighthearted...and eager to address a greeting card. Ken's middle son's birthday is coming up. He'll be tickled when he receives it.

My sorrow had been stamped out, at least for that day.

Closing PO BOX 6693

Lian Gouw

Shuffling toward the counter at the post office
I finger his PO Box keys in my pocket,
strangely happy for the line.

It's my turn.
I clutch the two brass keys hard in my fist,
pressing their imprints into my palms,
before sliding them off his silver keychain
with the Mercedes Benz emblem.

I push the keys across the worn counter,
watch the agent gather them in her hand.
Two dollar bills lie now
where the keys were before —
"Thank you."
I slip the key deposit into my wallet,
drive to the grocery store on auto pilot.
Two dollars – the end of nineteen years.

A head of lettuce, grapefruit,
zucchini, a loaf of bread.
The tab comes to $7.43.
I count the change out on the counter.

Take out a five...hesitate,
then take the two dollar bills from my billfold.
"Here," I say, placing them in the checker's hand.
"This will do it."

Widowhood: Some Notes (Part 2)

Cathy Douglas

I hear you talking behind me; still,
your flirting patter doesn't fall on my ear
with the weight of my dead husband's whisper.

For all my soul knows
he could have died yesterday,
and the day before been our wedding day.

One day of forever,
of cake and champagne and lovemaking,
of consecrating our home and blessing the children.

I'm sure you're not a bad person,
it's just that I've nothing to say to you,
occupied as I am as a dead man's wife.

level, the creative process and the healing process arise from a single

Pruning Time

Becky Haigler

They pruned the trees last week;
cut down the twisted one
that looked like lovers standing toe to toe
but pulling back at arms' length;
cut it down ten inches below the ground
and carved it into kindling.

You hadn't wanted to let them do it.
"It's too cold; too wet," you said.
"They'll have to take down the fence."
What did you think they would cut away
with the years of random branching
and the rotting hammock?

There are still two trees
beside the house where we spent
twenty of our thirty years together.
They are pruned bare and awkward just now;
no grace of green to cover
their needy waiting for Spring.

Passersby can see them, separate,
on either side of the path.

source. When you are an artist, you are a healer; a wordless trust of the

One holds an empty birdhouse
making a silent "Oh!" in the cold.
They cannot see the roots
holding hands underground.

Notices

Sharon Ellison

...died January 21...
services pending with...
I read the words, but I...numb
Does reading make it feel real?

...born on April 26, 19...
Chicago...son of...USAF...
H-SU...employed by...husband...
father...brother...grandfather...
...memorials in honor to...
Truth, yet I...numb
Does that make it feel real?

Funeral service today...
at...church; burial afterward...
...cemetery Garden of Meditation...
Going through the motions...
...yearning to cry out...numb
Tell me it's not real...please...

Grandpa's Shoes

Sheryl L. Nelms

when he died
we gave
away

all of his clothes

but the shoes
Grandma could not
stand to
touch

she left them
had me

sack them

in brown
Safeway bags

"Take them out somewhere,"
she said

"Don't tell me where."

It's All About Balance

Mary Pfeiffer

When my grandmother reached a healthy 100, I calculated that she had lived twenty-two of those years as a widow. I considered how many new shoes it would take to help me through the grief of outliving my husband and told him to increase his life insurance. I would need more than my inherited "nothing can get the better of me" stoicism to live without him. He couldn't argue. His family didn't have anyone in the race beyond 78.

We had a balanced marriage. I worried about spending pennies. He didn't bother with amounts after the decimal point and thought the bank was always right. In early marriage, I took charge of finances.

With a union as good as ours, promising 'til death do us part posed no threat. We couldn't even imagine the "D" word putting our marriage asunder or that God would halt our fun.

When my husband inconveniently died before we had our retirement planned, the roof leak fixed, or the movie chosen for that Saturday night, I moved all of the household files to the dining table. Some years before, having developed a nervous

children know, it is above all by the imagination that we achieve per-

tic from watching the bank balance try to flatline, I had yielded bookkeeping to him. Now, taking over his system was like a lefty trying to cut with right-handed scissors. What I immediately needed was a trustworthy bookkeeper, an organizer to convert everything to my method – whatever that was. No one applied. Months into my new life, my dad told a friend who asked how I was doing that he thought I would be okay...if I ever got the dining table cleared off.

My excuse: after working all day, lethargy over-whelmed me at home. Besides, if anyone cared to notice, emails at work inundated me. Not about work, about others in my school community be-coming widows. Five months into my new life, a "We are saddened to learn..." message blinked on my computer. Gerry's husband lived a week after his heart attack. We belonged to the same teacher organization. Her daughter had been in my eighth grade class. I waited until after the funeral to call her.

Expecting to offer sympathy but little else, I was surprised that we talked for hours. Gerry missed their Friday night movies. It sounded simple when I proposed seeing a movie together. Before con-tacting her to suggest that first evening, I paced like a sixteen-year-old phoning for his first date. What if she didn't want to join me? What if I were bothering her? What if she wanted to be left alone? I avoided the directness of the phone and emailed her. Our shy emails went back and forth until we found a free Friday.

With awful regularity, more district messages announced each new widow. Marilyn had car-pooled to graduate school with me. Gwen lived four doors down my street. A friend introduced me to Verlene and left her in my care. Lynne...Norma... Jane...Judy.

I decided I couldn't spend the second half of my life going to work, going home; going to church, going home; encouraging other widows, circling the dining table. I comforted myself with cookies and tea, my drugs of choice. That restored the lost grief pounds and told friends I was "over the mourning."

I tried a grief support class. At my first session, I heard someone from the far end of the table mention that his house painting was finished. Without waiting for introductions, I called in that direction, "Do you know a good painter? I'm looking for one." I left with the recommendation on a napkin and a place at their dinner table the next week.

Someone tired of TV dinners suggested we eat together regularly. Tuesday dinners soon included Saturday breakfasts and then Thursday evening cards. We ate, advised one another about probate, and commiserated over flat tires. We wondered if we would be able to read again or if we were losing our minds. Cecil, an outrageous flirt, made the women feel special. Beauford diagnosed automobile pings and knocks. Women offered cooking tips. When Bill despaired over his wife's empty opera seat, we all bought tickets and took turns sitting beside him.

At first my daughters left worried messages if their phone calls didn't find me at home. "Mom, where are you? I've called twice." That changed to a resigned, "I guess you're out with 'Your Group.'"

My turn to host card games came on a day I had my furnace and air conditioner inspected. The serviceman, looking more distraught than the ER doctor who delivered my bad news, told me I needed repairs before cold weather – to the tune of $10,000. That evening, I served the three men in the group hot-from-the-oven cherry pie then invited them to my attic to see my furnace. The property manager helped himself to a second slice and promised to send his serviceman over the next day. The repairs cost $1000.

Well-meaning voices continued to interrupt at work. "We thought you might want to call Glenna, over in Library Media Services. Her husband passed away this week."

Out loud I mumbled an appropriate reply. Silently, I carped, *I've never heard of her and I'm not calling her. I'm full up with cheerleading the widow squad.*

I had taken to venting to Alter Ego. Sometimes, she chose the silent route of a tolerant husband. More often, she argued with my unreasonable

a heartache no one can heal, love leaves a memory no one can steal."

attitudes by pinging my conscience with unrelenting reminders to play nice.

Within the month, God transferred Glenna to my office. After another month, Glenna joined Marilyn and me for our first girls' trip. People began calling us the "School Marms" and leaving a wide swath around us, lest what we had was catching.

I told my widows about the therapy group that had given me back my sanity. Some joined. At monthly sessions, speaker after speaker counseled us to, "Start new traditions." Each suggestion raised a topic for discussion.

"Be good to yourself and get massages," brought on giggles. Those too timid to try one at least benefitted from the laughter. The men passed on aromatherapy. We congratulated ourselves for forming our group of "W's."

At Christmastime, we balked. Except for those who had local grandkids, not one of us put up decorations. After Mavis Marvel gave her "How to Get through the Holidays" presentation, we soothed ourselves by grumbling about her. Easy for her to tell us to "Light a Memory Candle." That takes about 43 seconds even counting finding a match that will light. What about the other 23 hours and 17 seconds of Christmas Day?

For three Christmases I wallowed under *bah* and *humbug*. My house ignored the holidays. A few lights and the scent of pine might have been nice, but the work of putting it up and taking it down overwhelmed me. I felt glum. Then guilty. So I dragged out the excuse that I spent from Christmas through New Years miles away with my extended family. The rest of the group, however, should make their houses festive.

I pressured, "We should step out of our widows' weeds and take part in festivities."

I confessed: "After singing in my church Christmas concert, I hate returning alone to a dreary house." It sounded like a new recruit at AA.

I bribed: "The rest of us will come and look if you decorate."

No one made a move to start that new memory.

The following year I capitulated – with conditions. I would pull Christmas boxes down from the attic. BUT they must sit through my concert and afterward come to my house. More than a dozen came. They wore gaudy sweaters and laughed. We comforted ourselves with food. The next year and the next, the party grew. I had started a tradition.

The day I dumped the files on the dining table, I planned to never smile again. Fear said that if I started to enjoy life as a "W," everyone would dismiss that perfect union I boasted about. Now I'm shepherding new widows – without qualification or license. I revel in faces lit with shared joy on nights when they crowd my home. Our Saturday laughter puzzles waiters who wonder why we don't act sad. People seem to envy how much fun The Group

the most welcome and efficient consolation to the afflicted. Said a wise

enjoys. They envy – as long as they don't have to join us.

When family eyes my always-in-progress financial pile, I grouse about having no time.

"You might get your work done if you'd cut back on your social life with The Group." My daughters are starting to sound mother-like.

"Or," Alter Ego is pinging again, "you can skip balancing that checkbook and gain an extra hour per month." She is becoming my new best friend. "The bank says you have enough for a pair of shoes."

ritual

Phyllis Wax

you are not here,
I know, yet
a stone lodges
in my throat
like the one I place
on the granite marker –
a calling card –
I was here
you were not

forgotten

man to one in deep sorrow, "I did not come to comfort you; God only can

Morning, Third Sunday in June

Phyllis Wax

The call comes
as though planned
just as I cut into a yolk
"Hi, Mom"

and on the horizon
I see a scrap of sail

I know better
than to say "My eggs
are getting cold, can I call you back?"
because her voice has the scent
of a cloud, a wisp of the wind
which is pushing the sail closer

Casually we share our weekend
but soon there is no more to say – after all
we spoke just yesterday

On the water
the sail luffs,
a voice warns
"Coming about"

do that; but I did come to say how deeply and tenderly I feel for you

"Happy Father's Day"
she says, "Thanks for being both"

The yolk is a loud lump
upon my plate

Guided by the Having

Carol Ayer

I breathe in air of tears,
eat slices of pungent grief.
I embody sorrow.

But you have taught me well,
my darling.
One truly doesn't know
how to love
until that love is lost.

One day, some day,
I will fall in love again.
Even then, I will think of you,
and be guided by the having.

Keep Watering

Phyllis Wax

Sometimes it seems the heart
keeps beating
after the soul is gone.

The body performs its daily tasks,
breathes in, breathes out, breathes in
though the green within
is shrivelled and limp.

Arms move, legs move
only by rote. Skin is asleep to caress,
eyes oblivious to filled sails or full moon,
nose and tongue numb to the pleasure
of peonies, summer corn, of sweet wine.
The body is there, yet
not there.

But the day comes when a tendril
sprouts and the heart turns
toward the sun.

Outside, in the untended garden,
the pale apricot poppy, the lush
purple iris, all the scrambled wildflowers
persevere.

It's a Date!

Carol McAdoo Rehme

"Should I meet him there Saturday night?" she asked.

"Of course not, you know the family rule," I said. The cold pork chops hissed against the sizzling skillet. *"Your date must always —"*

"It is not a date," she interrupted.

"...come right to the door," I chanted without missing a beat. We had rehearsed this very conversation before. A slight pause followed. "Where is he taking you?"

"Out for supper and maybe somewhere afterwards." Panic peppered her voice. "A whole evening together – alone. What will we talk about?"

"Knowing you, you'll talk about anything and everything. Since when have you been at a loss for words, anyway?" I joked, handing her a short stack of stoneware salad plates.

"But this is different. I hardly know Tom."

Brushing aside crisp kitchen curtains, I peered into the deepening dusk. A gentle rain blurred the boundaries, skewing the scene like a photograph out of focus. "Well, there's always the weather.

Better yet, get him to talk about himself. Ask your boyfriend —"

"He is not my boyfriend."

"... about his interests. And, by the end of the date —"

"It's not a date!"

"...you'll know each other better and probably have lots to say," I encouraged. After all, I was experienced with this mother/daughter thing. I had raised four teenagers – all at one time – in the not-so-distant past. Could this be much different?

"Well – if you're sure." She paused. "It's just that..."

"Yes?" I coaxed, a little impatient with her hesitancy, my mind racing ahead to the details of dinner.

But the voice that answered had slowed, softened, and deepened.

"Do you realize, how long it's been?" Her words hung there. Suspended, unsupported in the sudden silence. Reaching across me to the stove, she flipped the pork chops and turned down the heat.

"How long it's been," she cleared her throat, "since I've dated, I mean? Not years. Decades. Decades! With your dad gone so long now, I think – maybe – well – maybe it's time. Why, Carol, I was seventeen the last time I went on a date."

I turned – once again a daughter – and winked. "Oh, but, Mom...remember? It's *not* a date!"

Bouncing Back

Stephen Gallup

For a period of time after my wife Judy died in 1994, a strange thing kept happening to me. Again and again, I found myself standing in the middle of a room, with absolutely no idea of what I had been doing, why I had gone there, or what I'd meant to do.

Up until that point, Judy's long illness had kept me busy. For two years, she'd had frequent medical appointments and hospitalizations, moments of which still remain vivid in my memory.

For example, there was the rainy day when I found myself running at top speed behind her wheelchair, trying to get her from the car to the door of the clinic before she became soaked.

There were also the times when she seemed to be doing so well that recovery felt like a reasonable thing to hope for. She'd greet her doctors with such cheerfulness that they wondered if she might be "denying her symptoms." At home, there were also dark hours when all she knew was pain. I remember the way she looked at the clock when I gave her a pill. She knew it took twenty minutes for the medication to take effect, and she was steeling herself to hold on that long.

I tried to be emotionally supportive, while taking over aspects of family life that had previously been her domain. Then, abruptly, she was gone. And with her went almost all of my focus. Adrift, I remained in Busy mode, even with no real direction. There were still impulses to go and do something, but each time the notion faded away before I could do it. That was scary.

Fortunately, I did have other responsibilities. Judy and I had a son, who happened to be disabled. Joseph relied on me for his care. I also still had a job, and definitely needed the income. These two concerns distracted me from my grief. They kept me involved with other matters.

Almost two decades have passed since those days, and I look back on them now with wonder. Every time one of my friends loses a loved one, I see that same confusion and doubt. Whether the death was expected or not, the survivor enters a period of stunned bewilderment. Things stop making sense. There seems to be no point to continuing. Then, gradually, out of the fog, questions take form.

Is my life over, too? Can I even make this adjustment? Is any more fun for me even possible? The answers to these questions are no, yes, and emphatically yes. The loss of a spouse, no matter how dear, does indeed close an important phase of one's life. However, that loss does not mean it's time to give up. We are still here, and I think it's safe to say that we're here for a reason. Reasons tend to become apparent in due course.

In the meantime, there are things a recently widowed individual can do to ease the transition back into an active life. This could be a very detailed list, I think, but for now let's focus on the high points. I'm sure you will have heard these before. However, I can vouch for them. They worked for me.

Get involved in something.

What sort of activities or causes have been important to you in the past? It's possible that you may have changed so that they have lost their appeal, but consider those things first. If these activities involve interaction with other people, so much the better. For most, if not all of us, this is a time for human contact.

If familiar activities just don't excite you now, consider stepping out and trying something quite different.

In my case, traveling to China was something I had always imagined doing, although I'd never thought it would actually happen. In the year after Judy died, I resumed a long-discontinued study of the Chinese language. I played language tapes in the car while driving around town, and rented Chinese movies to watch at night. At the end of that year, I actually went to China on a solo vacation. I saw the Great Wall and the Forbidden City, and I had lots of opportunities to find out if I could make myself understood there. Once, riding on a crowded bus, next to a young Chinese father with a crying baby, I succeeded in distracting the child and entertaining it for the rest of the trip. I really felt proud of myself for being able to do that. Every day of the time I spent there was a great adventure. I felt as if I were suddenly leading a different life.

Expect good things. Expect wonderful things.

A lot has been said about the way optimism attracts good outcomes. Emotions like gloom and self-pity might be easier, but they have the opposite effect. And there's really no justification for them. Yes, we've lost someone very, very important, someone who can never be replaced. But would that person want us to spend our remaining days in sorrow? Not likely! Our spouses loved us and surely would have wanted continuing fulfillment in our lives.

My wife Judy died in a November. As the end of that year approached, I became serious about making some New Year's resolutions. In addition to my son's ongoing needs, my employer was making it clear that layoffs were coming. In fact, the company was shutting down operations altogether. I had to get active and find a new source of income. Those were my top two priorities, but I ended up with a list of five or six objectives that I held in mind as I went about my life every day. I reviewed that list morning and night, and monitored my progress. That list gave me a purpose.

thirst to the pot." George Herbert ~§~ "Grief is Newark. It's there.

One item further down the list was the wish to expand my social life. In those days, of course, I had no thought of remarrying. That kind of relationship was beyond my expectations. However, because I did anticipate good things, a new partner came my way. And as a result of that new union, I now find myself, at this late stage in my life, with two more children. I've gone from grieving spouse to a dad who helps kids with their homework and school projects. It has been a very long time since I've had to solve quadratic equations or drill someone on spelling words or the parts of speech. These tasks keep me young and tuned in to this changing world. Because of his disability, Joseph never needed that kind of support. However, he seems glad to participate, at least as a spectator, in all this new activity. We've been very fortunate, and I'm quite sure Judy would be glad.

Everyone who has been widowed has a unique story, but I daresay these two points figure in most of them. How do we carry on? Let us count the ways.

Her Candle

Carl Palmer

I've got so many candles that I've never burned—
a marriage candle
a first communion candle from one of the kids
a bicentennial candle
a millennium candle
so many candles that I've never burned
Yet her candle I've burned for over twenty years
not every day but most everyday
a memory of what once was
of what we'd had
we – me and her
her candle
originally voluptuously large
beautifully ornate
burning bright hot and fast
we were young then
Gradually her candle became hollow
with most of the outside still holding fast
dusty with age
the wick long lost
hollowness temporarily filled
with a tealight candle
certain songs movies or moods

seem to rekindle the freshness
remind me of when her candle was new
In the light of day reality blazes
her candle actually a hollow shell
so hard to visualize as it once was
as in last night's memory
beginning to wonder
continuing to wonder
if after all this time
I shouldn't just throw it out
this foolish vigil
this senseless old man
end this memorial
this ritual and move on
But as the room grows dark
the many candles that I've never burned
remain so
a new tea candle
and she is back
we – me and her
her candle
and my thoughts
of twenty years ago

Comforter

Becky Haigler

Before I met you,
I didn't have to fight anybody for the covers.
Back when I slept alone,
I controlled the electric blanket.
And when you weren't here,
I could get up in the morning
And tuck in one corner
And the bed was made.

Before I met you,
I could sleep smack in the middle of the bed.
Back when I slept alone,
Nobody cared if I snored.
And when you weren't here,
I could sit up against the pillows
And read until midnight
And eat crackers in bed.

Before I met you,
My feet were always cold at night.
Back when I slept alone,
I had to have a light on.
And now that you're not here,

There is no one to curl up around me
And kiss my neck
And say, "I love you."

Over morning coffee, my mother told me
Judy Callarman

I saw your father last night,
in a dream. He was young and slim
and wore his Navy uniform.

Where have you been so long,
I said. He took my hand
and said *On a long journey.*

The edges were fading.
I said Do you have to go back —
can I go with you?

He said *yes.*

It's January Again

Lian Gouw

It's January again.
Dreary rainy days,
cold, howling winds.

Like last year,
poplar and elm stand in gold,
liquid amber sets the world aflame.
Like last year,
I make springrolls
serve them at the dinner
I make him on the seventh
day of every month.
Like last year
I sit with him.

Now incense spirals
waft across his plate.

This morning
I took this year's
first daffodils
to the cemetery.

Introduction to Widowhood

Anna Florio

In November of 2011 I joined the universal club of widows. Unlike most clubs its members did not join voluntarily. It's one of those clubs you get drafted into ready or not. Of course no matter how much advance notice you get, you are never really ready. As a new member I find I have a lot of questions about this. Some of which are:

1) When do you learn to get on with life without your husband/best friend?
2) When does it begin to get easier/ or does it?
3) When do you stop looking for or inventing reasons to get up each morning?

There is one advantage to this club: its members seem to be more than willing to help you find your way. They, unlike most other people, do not say "I'm sorry" or ask how you are doing. They don't have to. They know from experience how you are doing. Instead they teach by example. They show you by living their lives to the fullest, things do get better. They are there if you need to talk and are the ones who tell you that you are not going crazy, what you are feeling and doing is normal and you will work it out in your own time.

As a group they have told me to take things at my own pace and to do only what I feel I can. They have advised me to take things as slow or as fast as I am comfortable doing. They have told me not to second guess any of what has happened but to understand I did everything I could. They remind me that he is truly in a better place and that his suffering has stopped.

What is most amazing is they seem to come from nowhere. They are neighbors that you barely spoke to before. They are women in church who notice you are upset and ask why. You even bump into them in supermarkets and drug stores. A simple word or statement and the conversations begin, as if the powers that be, God, is setting up the meetings. Another thing that amazes me is they seem as happy to meet you as you are them. These meetings seem to be mutually beneficial.

These strong women are truly members of a sisterhood. One I have joined sooner than I wanted to, but one day I hope I will be able to teach other new members by experience. However, for now I'm still learning from my sisters.

And I believe that love is stronger than death." Robert Fulghum ~§~

Winter Damage

Patsy Collins

I didn't want another day to begin, but what choice did I have? Once awake, I had to survive the hours until I could sleep again. I opened the curtains, not expecting light to flood into either the room or my life. Looking across the cold empty fields, I thought something was different. The broken oak tree was the same, the scars from winter's storm clearly visible. A limb had been torn away. The branch was gone; logs now on somebody's fire, but its loss will always be evident. The tree's shape is distorted, no longer perfect, no longer balanced. I felt for that tree; its pain was my pain. The tree and I were damaged forever.

The storm that took its finest branch stole my husband. He was a vet, called out to a cow having difficulty calving. He never reached the farm, but the cow lived, her calf, too. My husband was not so fortunate. Sheets of corrugated tin, wrenched from a farm building, lay lethally invisible, hidden by night and rain. My husband crashed on the way to the birth and died on the way to hospital.

I looked unseeing, at the tree, and newly ploughed acres. There was no barley yet, just cold

"Grief is the agony of an instant, the indulgence of grief the blunder of

wet earth and seeds waiting to germinate. The sun was shining, perhaps enough to tempt succulent shoots to push into cold spring air. There was not enough sun to cheer me; I doubted there would ever be enough sun.

I could see buildings – barns and sheds for the sheep and lambs. Everything looked as it had for months. Since the oak and I had suffered our loss, nothing had changed. Every sad empty day was a repeat of the one before. His family tried to comfort me, but they couldn't help. For us to be together without him is proof of our loss. They'll never get back their son. Perhaps one day they'll get back their daughter-in-law; but not yet.

There were happy days previously. I can barely recall them now. There was joy when we bought this cottage. We celebrated as if we'd bought not only a home, but also a happy future. We thought we'd purchased a lifetime of contentment; but no. There is no business deal that can secure hopes and dreams. These come freely when they please. I should have taken better care of mine; they were too easily broken. I'd loved him and known his love in return. Now I can't remember how that felt. I can't remember the happiness without realizing my loss afresh.

So I don't think about the past. I don't think about the future either. I try not to think at all; instead I concentrate on surviving. I cook and eat and clean. Life will get better with time. Others who've suffered similar loss assure me this is true. I believe them. Until then there is the temptation of combining my sleeping tablets with Duncan's whisky.

Duncan. I haven't said his name since the day they nailed his coffin shut. I spoke to him, whilst he lay cold and calm on the silk lining. I don't remember what I said, but talking comforted me a little. Then they shut him away from me. They took him to church and we all sang. Then they buried him. Now he's gone, I can no longer speak to him. He's not here beside me and he's not in the churchyard. He's in the past.

I'd not known before he died that I was pregnant. I'd guessed the truth in the weeks afterwards but wasn't sure. Grief has many effects on the body. I told no one. It wasn't the time to raise false hopes. Yesterday, the doctor confirmed I am indeed pregnant.

The aged oak tree blurs. Tears spill quietly from my eyes. Holding the windowsill for support, I allow sorrow to flow through me. Now the grieving has begun. It will eventually fade. Calmer again, I look out at the tree. Has it accepted its fate? Will it continue to grow, forming new branches to replace the old?

Something is different, and now I am certain it's not my tears making the tree seem less distinct.

I fetch Duncan's binoculars and focus on the branches. I see what is different, there is a softness to the twigs. Leaves are beginning to expand. The

a frozen river; most of the time he feels safe enough, but there is always

tree is producing new life. It will never be the same,
but it will recover. I put my hand onto my abdomen.
I haven't been eating much, yet still my belly feels
full and round. I will produce a new life and together
we shall have a future.

Death – Our Houseguest

Lian Gouw

He was a quiet kind of guy.
Not saying much,
not moving around,
screeching chairs, slamming doors.
Wrapped tightly in his cloak,
the visor of his cap pulled low,
he was a constant presence.

He ignored my pleas to leave.
Instead, he settled deeper in the easy chair.
Threatened to make his presence known
with shaking walls, collapsing roofs.
I bowed my head accepting his presence.
I cooked and cleaned to please him.
Catered to his every whim.
Rushing to his side at every rustle,
I begged, "Please stay quiet.
Until you take your leave, please, stay quiet."

For seven months and seven days
I was his handmaid.
Then, one evening,
he rose without a word.
Slid across the room,
turned the doorknob without a noise and left.
Under his cloak
he carried a heart.

Sleeping Alone

Glenda Beall

In the dark I close my eyes,
try to push away the memories,
the feel of your smooth skin
sliding over lean bones and strong sinew,
the softness of your hair, smelling clean as
fresh air and rainwater. It grew back thicker,
darker
after chemo.

Solitude

Glenda Beall

I've always needed time alone.
To gather meandering thoughts,
musings on life, mine and yours.
I snatched my moments
where I found them.
But now the stillness whispers to me.
Careful what you ask for.

Waking in our quiet house,
no one greets me with, "Hey, Hon,
Get me a cup of coffee, will ya?"
No one sits in your chair,
No one speaks but the dog.

Hours pass while I make
eggs and toast – no coffee –
not for one. Feed the dog
and cat, answer email, fewer
now it seems.

Slowly I learn to use the quiet,
to ponder my future, to cry
when I am stabbed with memories

so precious I can't bear the pain,
to face the hard reality that you
will not return.
I am alone inside the
silence that I craved.

Grief Haiku

Peggy Muir

He is so not there —
shadow man in the doorway —
the dead man I love

The widow's Oscar
is for the performance art
of acting alive.

Dickinson said that —
Hope is the thing with feathers.
Grief's the thing with teeth.

Would you really ask
a double amputee if
he "still" missed his legs?

I'll just go along,
we'll hold hands, enjoy the day.
Death as an outing.

The robin that's you
sat on the car's door handle
trying to get in

Wow! What a concept.
Go out and find a new love.
Life as a Walmart.

Clothes in a closet
Losing the lingering smell,
another death shock.

Somewhere in Vermont
is a high, grassy meadow
where we once made love.

I "got through" a year
to find endless years looming,
no survival prize.

The show "Survivor"
should star two teams of widows
overcoming grief

I play tetherball,
thrust the grief away from me
and it comes right back!

I've had a good day,
small and large gifts all around.
Can I go to bed?

Widows could power cities.
Striding ahead of the pain,
we'd have a real job.

The wedded are "One."
So what is the new sum
when one of "One" dies?

"Why me?" cried aloud
brings a voice with Bubbe's tone,
"Why NOT you, Pegele?"

No Mind a Whetstone

Frieda W. Landau

No mind a whetstone to my own
Allusions fly past uncaught
Pleasures of the mind
Pleasures of the body
Inextricably intertwined
Buried in your grave
Nothing to fill the now hollow place
Where Logos and Eros once danced with delight

---

doesn't hear her husband's ghost all the time, but only some of the time.

The First Night

Aline Soules

Our son drives home
to your dead body.

Five hours on the road —
just a teenager
alone in a car.

Will he see the truck
roaring past? The car
that cuts him off? The deer

startled and numb
in the middle of the road?

Will he stop to take a break?
Focus on pumping gas or
eating a cardboard burger —

anything not to think? But I
who had to call him
can't stop.

Her grief is replaced with a useful sadness." Jonathan Safran Foer ~§~

When We Became 1

Lavania Fritts

Today I meet with a realtor to sell this land. The thought of saying goodbye has been running through my head for weeks now. As I lean against the rusty red farm gate, balancing on the cattle guard, memories in golden bubbles surround me... float through me.

There is a message echoing in my brain that insists on being heard, not only heard, but accepted.

Tom is gone.

Tom has died.

The life I knew no longer exists.

Tom, my love, when I buried you, I buried us. Only an "I" is here. The I who has been trying to survive the shock, the grief of losing you.

Through the first year there was no choice but to deal with financial matters. To have your name removed and mine put in its place.

The second year there were so many "we's" to let go of, I could barely survive. I learned to detest the word "widow." What do widows do? How do widows act? There is no comfort in going out with our old friends. I am half of a couple. The unease is mine. I was eighteen when we married and became a twosome, a "we." I always had something going in the artsy world and you in your engineering job.

"Honey, you go to the opera. Just please, please don't make me go."

"Sweetheart, I am so glad you can design computers. Let's just hope I can learn how to use one."

Friends saying, "Are you going to let him do that? Is Tom going to let you do that?" What do you mean let me? Different sides of the brain merging, loving, supporting, never boring.

We had so many plans. This land I am standing on is one of them.

"Honey, wait until you see the land I found. Put your boots on."

We pulled up to an old broken-down wooden gate, leaning almost to the ground. We didn't need to worry about breaking in. We sprayed for ticks and chiggers and started walking down to the pond that never went dry, to the west with its view of downtown, on south into a grove of trees that revealed a rock ledge with a view of a lush green valley covered in a soft mist. This is where we sat down to still ourselves, to breathe in the quietness of nature. God's creation. The clear smell of Mother Earth. Arms around each other, we became one with the stillness.

A doe with her fawn looked at us from the trees. A rustling behind us. Two black snakes, heads swaying, checking us out, then lying back down on their heated rock. Squirrels ran up and down trees. We had been accepted. Oh, the flights of fancy we

ing, and the dead know it not." Xenophon ~§~ "Few of us will forget

saw in our heads, as we sat on the rocks. We rose quietly and walked softly to the north front of the property, only to find a strange-looking ditch. The owner had told Tom it was part of an old buffalo wallow. Buffalo had roamed here. Indians had hunted here. Prairie grass. It had never been plowed under. It was as it had always been. Our minds saw Indians hidden by the trees, painted for the hunt, sitting deathly still on their ponies waiting for the signal to raise their bows. The sound of a war cry still in the air. This is Osage Indian land. They still own the mineral rights.

We bought the land that day. It had called to us. It was ours. We met with the builder, planning our dream home. How we loved this land. The city denied our water tap and we couldn't get water. There was a moratorium on the water line. Appealing to the city council, getting a lawyer, all to no avail. We were crushed. No dream home, but the land remained. When we needed a place to contemplate, to picnic, to embrace, we came to our land. We could never let it go. Even when we moved to another state we kept the land. One day we would go back. The land would always know us.

I glide in my golden bubble of memories with you beside me, remembering.

All of the usual platitudes came pouring in from friends and family who love us.

God's will be done. One day you will understand. God only gives you what you can handle. Be strong. God knows you can do this. Well good for God because I don't understand it.

I'm mad.

I'm sad.

I don't want to be an *I*.

I liked the *we* that sat together at church, in the movies holding hands, watching our children grow. I miss the loving embraces, the heat of your body keeping my feet warm at night, the sharing of life. I knew how to be a *we*. But this *I* is unsure of herself. She stumbles, she falls, she cries

I tell myself that the years of being a *we* with you has made me strong and I will find my way through this. A new path will appear. But what I really want to do is to stand in the middle of this land and howl with the coyotes. Let all hear my mourning. Like a dark cloak covering the villain in a melodrama, this grief covers me. Suffocates me. My heart so heavy in my chest I cannot breathe. Sobs choke me.

My golden bubbles start floating away. I had really planned to walk this land saying goodbye, but I have changed my mind. I had rather climb back into my golden bubble with the memories of this land forever kept with you beside me.

I put the heavy chain back around the post, close the lock, and as the chain rattles down the rusty post, I walk to the car. I turn back for one last look, for it is only I who stands here. Only an *I* crying. And this *I* is so alone.

when the Indians returned to it and recognized their slaughtered war-

House Guest

Mary Cleary Krauss

Anger walks in the door
and sits in the best chair
I ignore him
I know I'm unexpected, he says
but grief and I travel together
He's embarrassed by me
Never includes me in conversation
Get used to me

I'll be here awhile
We'll bump into each other
on a regular basis
I heard you slam that door
saw you kick dirt on his grave
Don't fret
it's people like you who keep me healthy
Nice place you got here.

Easter Oasis

Julie Stuckey

my felt smile
arose from unexpected
remembrance
of shared laughter
(was that a lifetime ago?)
now as I carry within me
your essence, your being
fine threads of connection
sustain me through weary days
of heaviness.
biding time
searching for balance
keening in my off-kilter world
for you
grappling with incompleteness
needing you
desperately clinging to our
intimate place in the world —
my oasis…

while the desert around me scorches.

Creeping Through the Horseradish
Thelma Zirkelbach

"To a worm in horseradish, the whole world is horseradish." Yiddish proverb

To a widow, especially a new one, the whole world is widowhood.

Grocery shopping: The first time you're at the supermarket, it hits you. You're shopping for one now. How much to buy? All those other carts you pass are so full. Yours, not so full. And do you want to cook anyway? Your new world doesn't lend itself to gourmet food, new recipes. Everything tastes like cardboard. Maybe you'll buy a few frozen dinners and be done with it. Or stop at McDonalds and pick up a Happy Meal. (There's an oxymoron for you. Meals are no longer happy when you're eating alone). But wait. Frozen dinner and fast food, Happy Meal or Whopper, will just make you feel more alone. Who knew sitting across the table from someone could mean so much? You never gave it much thought when it was an everyday occurrence.

Going to bed: Another decision. Stay on "your" side, move to the middle, sleep on "his" side because maybe you'll feel closer to him that way? Personally, I've never moved an inch away from my side.

Everything in your life seems suddenly connected to your new status. The toilet seat is always down now. You can't fasten a favorite necklace. I once woke a neighbor because I couldn't unfasten one. My burglar alarm once started beeping because its battery was low. Even with a ladder, I couldn't reach it. I swallowed my pride, marched across the street and introduced myself to a new neighbor. I hadn't met her yet, but I'd noticed she was tall.

You see a couple standing shoulder to shoulder in line at the movies or an elderly couple strolling hand in hand toward the park. A stab of pain and envy hits you. Why couldn't that be you and your husband? Why don't you belong to someone, with someone any more?

Those people at your office or in your book club, complaining about their spouses, they don't realize how lucky they are. Or how their complaints hurt. You want to tell them, but you keep quiet. They wouldn't understand.

But gradually some of the pain dissipates, maybe after months or years. Oh, it still comes back at times, surprising you with its intensity. You hear a song, pass a restaurant you used to love, see a couple you used to go out with, but they don't include you any more.

You've begun to make a new life. Not because you want to, but because you must. Another Yiddish proverb says, "When one must, one can," and you've taken it to heart. New friends, new interests, bigger fasteners put on those old necklaces. You struggle out of the horseradish, and suddenly you can see the sky.

About the Authors

Nina Abnee lives and works in Chicago. She has been in advertising, working at Chicago's largest agency, Leo Burnett, for more than 25 years. She is the single parent of two adult daughters and two cock-a-poo pups. She is just beginning to write in her spare time and does her best thinking while walking the dogs. She aspires to expand her writing into a book about her new perspective on marriage.

Carol Ayer's poetry has been published by *Poetry Quarterly, Poesia, Every Day Poets*, and in previous Silver Boomer Books titles. Her other credits include *Woman's World, The Christian Science Monitor,* and several *Chicken Soup for the Soul* volumes. Carol lives in Northern California, and works as a freelance writer. Visit her website at *www.carolayer.com*.

Glenda Beall lives in Hayesville, North Carolina, where she teaches writing at her home studio, Writers Circle. Her poetry chapbook, *Now Might as Well be Then*, was published by Finishing Line Press three months after her husband's death in 2009. She has published poetry, non-fiction, short stories and writes articles for newspapers. Her poem, "No Safe Place," has been published in three online journals and will appear in two anthologies this year. Besides writing and teaching, Beall speaks on the dangers of indoor air pollution in our homes, schools and workplaces. One of her poems was published in *Freckles to Wrinkles*, a Silver Boomer Books anthology. She blogs at *www.Glenda-CouncilBeall.blogspot.com* and *www.ProfilesAndPedigrees.blogspot.com*.

"Grief is perhaps an unknown territory for you. You might feel both

Susanne Braham is an editor for the Publications Office at Columbia University. She began writing poetry as a means of catharsis following the sudden death of her 56-year-old husband in 2002. She has a Bachelor's degree from Columbia in English and comparative literature and a Master's degree from Emerson College in theater education.

Cathy Bryant held many jobs, including civil servant, life model and nanny, before becoming a writer. Now her poems and stories have been published all over the world in magazines and anthologies. In 2009 Cathy was runner-up in the *Woman & Home* fiction prize; in 2010 she won the Marple Humourous Poetry Prize; in 2011 she was runner-up in several writing contests; and in 2012 she won the Swanezine Poetry Competition. Cathy co-edits *Best of Manchester Poets* and her collection *Contains Strong Language and Scenes of a Sexual Nature* came out in 2010. She lives in Manchester, United Kingdom.

Judy Callarman lives in Cisco, Texas. She is a retired professor of creative writing and English at Cisco College and chair of the Fine Arts Division. Her poems and nonfiction have won contests and been published in Silver Boomer Books' *This Path* and *From the Porch Swing; Radix; Passager; Grandmother Earth;* and *Patchwork Path – Christmas Stocking.* She is a Silver Boomer Books guest editor for the anthology *A Quilt of Holidays.*

Kathe Campbell lives her dream on a Montana mountain with her mammoth donkeys, a Keeshond, and a few kitties. Three children, eleven grands and three greats round out her herd. She is a prolific writer on Alzheimer's, and her stories are found on many ezines. Kathe is a contributing author to the *Chicken Soup For The Soul* and *Cup of Comfort* series, numerous anthologies, *RX for Writers,* magazines and medical journals. kathe@wildblue.net.

helpless and hopeless without a sense of a 'map' for the journey." Anne

K. Marguerite Caronna is a teacher, hopefully retiring soon so she can devote more time to her writing projects, including a novel set in a women's jail, and a script. Her writing life includes *Perspectives* pieces for the local NPR station, a script produced for TV and runner up winner of the Chistell Short Story Writing Contest. She never turns down an opportunity to travel.

Patsy Collins lives on the south coast of England. Her stories and poems have been published in a range of United Kingdom, Irish and Australian magazines including *Woman's Weekly, The Weekly News, Woman's Day, That's Life!* and *My Weekly.* Patsy is the author of two novels, *Escape to the Country* and *Paint Me a Picture.* She'd like you to visit her blog *Patsy-Collins.blogspot.com.*

Robyn Conley, the book doctor, speaks and writes about writing, editing, and marketing what you write. Her books include: *Insights from the Jobsite* published by Eagle Wings Press imprint of Silver Boomer Books; *Be Your Own Book Doctor,* which gives a checklist of editing tips for writers; and *What Really Matters to Me*, a journal that helps people discover their goals, and then offers practical tips to make those dreams come true. Her other published titles include a diversity of topics, such as *Beyond the Branches, Writing and Scrapping Your Complete Family Tree* and *Pray the Bible with Paper and Pen.* Her biographies include: *John Grisham, Cartoonists, Alexander G. Bell,* and the juvenile reference books: *Meerkats; Depression; Motion Pictures;* and *The Automobile.* Robyn has sold to major magazines, such as *The Writer, Writer's Digest, ABA: Student Lawyer,* and a score of others.

Carole Creekmore, a Baby Boomer who grew up in North Carolina, is a widow with two adult children, two grand-daughters, and an English Bulldog. With degrees in English from Wake Forest University, she teaches English, Creative

Writing, and Humanities at Georgia Perimeter College in the Atlanta area. She enjoys writing, traveling, genealogy, photography, and new adventures.

Barbara Darnall, the daughter of a high school English teacher and a West Texas lawyer and rancher, has been surrounded by words all her life and grew up telling stories and writing scripts for her playmates to perform. She graduated from Baylor University with B.A. and M.A. degrees in drama, and taught at the college level for several years. Immediate past-president of Abilene Writers Guild, she writes poetry, articles, and personal narratives, and has written and directed numerous short dramas for her church. She has copyedited one book and several manuscripts, and has published stories and poems in six previous Silver Boomer Books anthologies. As a tax consultant for more than thirty years, she particularly enjoys the letter-writing contests she occasionally gets into with the IRS!

Gail Denham's short stories, poetry, news articles, nonfiction, and photos have appeared for over thirty years in numerous magazines, books, anthologies, and on calendars and brochures. Denham has released three poetry chapbooks and leads writing workshops. Currently, poetry takes the forefront in her work. Although Denham thanks God she has not experienced widowhood, friends deal with that grief. It's Denham's wish to console and offer hope. "Gone? Not Really" was written for Denham's Aunt Esther after her dear husband, Uncle George, passed away suddenly. Aunt Esther takes this poem out frequently, reads it, and remembers.

Cathy Douglas lives in Madison, Wisconsin, where she works at a metaphysical shop and lives with one of her two grown sons. She enjoys writing a little bit of everything: poems, short stories, articles for the store newsletter and other nonfiction. She also has several novels in various

"I believe...that laughter is the only cure for grief. And I believe that

stages of disrepair. When she isn't working or writing, you'll usually find her outside – running, biking, kayaking, or just messing around in her garden. Her website is *cathydouglas.net.*

June Rose Dowis reads, writes and resides in Shreveport, Louisiana. A love of nature, a heart for the underdog, and a slice of everyday life find their way into her poetry that is divided equally between contemporary style and haiku. Her essays have been published in *Birds & Blooms, Appleseeds, Byline,* and *Shreveport Voices.* Her poetry has been published in *Ouachita Life* and anthologies, *From the Porch Swing, This Path, The Harsh and the Heart* and *Harbingers of Hope in Hard Times.* She was also a winner of the Highway Haiku contest in Shreveport with her haiku gracing a billboard.

Milton P. Ehrlich is an eighty-year-old psychologist who has published numerous poems in periodicals such as the *Antigonis Review, Toronto Quarterly Review, Rutherford Red Wheelbarrow, Shofar Literary Journal, Dream Fantasy International, Christian Science Monitor,* and *The New York Times.*

Terri Elders, LCSW, lives near Colville, Washington. She's a frequent contributor to anthologies, with over fifty pieces of creative nonfiction appearing in books such as *Chicken Soup for the Soul, Thin Threads* and *God Makes Lemonade.* She currently is a co-creator and editor for Publishing Syndicate's new anthology series, *Not Your Mother's Book.* A public member of the Washington State Medical Quality Assurance Commission, Terri received UCLA's 2006 Alumni Award for Community Service for her work with Peace Corps. She's lived in Belize, Guatemala, Dominican Republic and Seychelles. She blogs at *atouchoftarragon.blogspot.com.*

Sharon Ellison is a medical office manager who enjoys singing, playing piano and spending time with her grandchildren. In her spare time, she enjoys writing and has been published in *Proceedings* and *Nostalgia* magazines, as well as in four other Silver Boomer Books anthologies.

James Escher, a poet in East Central Illinois, is struggling to get a handle on aging gracefully. His work has most recently appeared in the *Pitkin Review* and is scheduled to appear in upcoming issues of the *Lost & Found Quarterly*. He balances writing with fatherhood, husbandhood, workinghood, and exhaustedhood.

Gretchen Fletcher's poems in her second chapbook, *The Scent of Oranges: poems from the tropics*, are set in South Florida where she lives and suffers from wanderlust. Fortunately, poetry allows her to travel for readings, book signings, and award ceremonies, the most exciting of which was in Times Square where she read her winning poem in the Poetry Society of America's Bright Lights/Big Verse competition.

Anna Florio is a retired high school language arts teacher. When it looked like cancer was going to win the battle her husband was fighting she retired to stay home with him. She has a daughter and two grandsons. She reluctantly joined the widows club in November of 2011. Like many members of this club she lost her best friend when she lost her husband. This loss prompted her to write as a way of expressing her emotions. Anna was born in Brooklyn, lived over twenty years in Queens, and now lives on Long Island.

Angie Francis found herself suddenly single at fifty, after the unexpected death of her husband of thirty years. Determined to make a new life, she left her job as nonprofit administrator, bought a ramshackle beach house on seven acres of land on the Chesapeake Bay, and began to study nonfiction writing. Her first book, *Wide Water View: Rebuilding a Life on the Chesapeake Bay*, is a memoir in progress. Ms. Francis now makes her home in Colorado, where she continues to study nonfiction writing and spends weekdays at her best job ever – part time nanny to grandsons Boyd and Zach.

Lavania Fritts, a native of Arkansas, honed her artistic skills in Bartlesville, Oklahoma as director of a summer arts program for teens. Performing with various choral and theatre groups, she has also served on several boards supporting the arts. Never content with one medium, Lavania is also a jewelry designer, painter, and partner in a construction company. One of her oil paintings currently graces the label of a very fine wine. Mother of two girls and a grandmother of three, she is following in the footsteps of a long line of storytellers. Putting the spoken word into print has become a passion in this next chapter of her life.

Joy Gaines-Friedler teaches creative writing for non-profits in the Detroit area including Springfed Arts Literary Arts program and Common Ground – a mental health core provider service. Both her poetry and prose are widely published in literary magazines including, *RATTLE, The New York Quarterly, Driftwood* and others. Her first book of poetry *Like Vapor* was published by Mayapple Press, 2008. Visit her website: *www.joygainesfriedler.com* – and yes, the tiger is real.

Elaine L. Galit is an award-winning freelance writer. Her work has appeared in anthologies such as *Chicken Soup for the Volunteer's Soul, Women Forged in Fire,* and *Chicken Soup for the Working Woman's Soul.* She also co-authored three travel books and taught writing at the University of Houston – Cinco Ranch. As a featured author at a Texas Book Festival in Austin, she attended an author's

think of grief as sadness...but there's also this thorniness, these edges

coffee at the Governor's Mansion with Governor and Mrs. Rick Perry. Her more than 150 magazine and online and photo credits include *Writer's Digest, Cowboy Sports and Entertainment Magazine, Neighborhood America.com, Houston Generation Magazine,* and *Woman's World.*

Stephen Gallup's disabled grown son inspired his memoir, *What About the Boy?* Please visit *fatherspledge.com* for details. After losing his first wife to cancer, Stephen remarried and is now trying to be a good parent to a preteen girl and a boy in kindergarten.

Patricia L. Goodman is a widowed mother and grandmother. She spent her career raising, training and showing horses with her orthodontist husband, on their farm in Chadds Ford, Pennsylvania. She now lives on the banks of the Red Clay Creek in Delaware, where she enjoys hiking, photography and spending time with her family. Her poetry has been published in journals and online and she is putting the finishing touches on her first book. Much of her inspiration comes from the natural world she loves.

Peter D. Goodwin divides his time between the streets and vibrant clutter of New York City, and the remnants of the natural world along Maryland's Chesapeake Bay. His poems have been published in the anthologies *September eleven; Maryland Voices; Listening to The Water: The Susquehanna Water Anthology; Alternatives To Surrender; Wild Things – Domestic and Otherwise; This Path; and From The Porch Swing* as well as in various journals, including *Rattle, Memoir(and), River Poets Journal, Delaware Poetry Review, Yellow Medicine Review, Twisted Tongue, Poetry Monthly, Main Street Rag,* and *Anon.*

Lian Gouw's moving poems meticulously choreograph the journey of caring for her ex-husband during his battle with cancer. From the initial shock of diagnosis, through the painful settling with the past, the focus on what is truly important emerges from her heartfelt poems. Anyone who has wrestled with resolving an ambivalent relationship and gone through the struggle of helping someone find as peaceful a death as possible will find echoes in Gouw's words and images. She is the author of *Only A Girl,* an historical novel, published in English and Indonesian. See more at her website *www.liangouw.com.*

Judy Lee Green, Tennessee-bred and cornbread-fed, is an award-winning writer and speaker whose spirit and roots reach deep into the Appalachian Mountains. She has been published hundreds of times and received dozens of awards for her work. She often writes about her large colorful family, remembering humble beginnings as the source for much of her inspiration. Her work can be found in many publications including *Now and Then: The Appalachian Magazine, Passager, The Rambler, Anthology of New England Writers, Christian Woman, Southern Arts Journal, Relief, Ultimate Christian Living,* and various anthologies and seasonal collections. She is a *Chicken Soup* writer.

Alice King Greenwood has been writing poetry, stories, articles, and music since taking early retirement from school teaching more than twenty-five years ago. She draws her material from multifaceted personal experiences in travel, community involvement, and, most importantly, life with her large family of five children, twelve grandchildren, and twelve great-grands. Her writings have appeared in nearly five dozen publications.

Becky Haigler is a founding partner in Silver Boomer Books and author of the short story collection *Not so GRIMM: gentle fables and cautionary tales.* Retired from teaching Spanish in Texas public schools, Becky follows her husband Dave wherever his work takes him. She is a mother and grandmother and dabbler in arts and crafts of various kinds, though she prefers the term "Renaissance woman."

CJ Heck is a published poet, writer, blogger and children's author who lives in Pennsylvania with her partner, Robert Cosmar, also an author. She has three married daughters and nine grandchildren. CJ writes poetry for both children and adults, fiction and nonfiction short stories, memoirs, and essays. She also maintains a website for children and writes three blogs, one dedicated to Vietnam veterans – CJ is a Vietnam War widow. Her second book, a sequel, will be published next month. A prolific writer, CJ is working on her tenth children's book, a book of poetry, and a collection of short stories.

Kehaunani Hubbard started writing poems when she was eight years old, fashioning them after her favorite author, Shel Silverstein. Originally encouraged by her second grade teacher she continues to write many decades later. Now she focuses primarily on personal essays or creative nonfiction, which are submitted to the lucrative market of literary journals. She currently lives in Nashville, Tennessee.

Mary Cleary Krauss is a retired middle school teacher and is pleased to be a part of Silver Boomer Books publications. She previously appeared in *Silver Boomers, From the Porch Swing,* and *The Harsh and the Heart.* She writes her life stories and poetry and is busy enjoying retirement.

Frieda W. Landau is a semi-retired writer and a photographer. She and her husband, Alan, who was also a writer and photographer, worked together specializing in military topics. Their work has appeared in *Newsweek, US News & World Report,* and similar worldwide publications. After he died, most untimely, on Christmas Day, 2004, she started writing poetry. Her first collection came out in October, 2011. When she's not writing poetry, she's working on a science fiction novel and taking care of sixteen teddy bears and five plot bunnies.

Meta E. Lee is a retired school librarian. She held jobs in both Chicago and Ft. Lauderdale. Recently widowed, Meta shares her home with a Rhodesian Ridgeback and a frisky cat. She enjoys spending time with her eleven grandchildren and three great grandchildren. Since her retirement Meta has been involved in creative writing. Her works, short stories and poetry, have been published in a variety of literary magazines. Meta is an active member of the Broward County Storytellers' Guild. She performs for children as well as adults. Her repertoire includes original works as well as traditional tales.

Maura MacNeil is the author of the poetry chapbook *A History of Water* (Finishing Line Press, 2007). Her poetry and prose has appeared in numerous publications and has been anthologized in *The Breath of Parted Lips: Voices from the Frost Place, Volume II* (CavanKerry Press), and *Shadow and Light: A Literary Anthology on Memory* (Monadnock Writers Group). She is co-founder and editor of *Entelechy International: A Journal of Contemporary Ideas*. Nominated four times for the Pushcart Prize, she lives in New Hampshire and is a professor of writing at New England College.

Marissa McNamara is an English professor in Atlanta, Georgia. She works to convince students that words, as poems or songs or essays, can be powerful. She writes poetry because she needs to convince herself that she is real. She writes poetry because she wants to convince others that they are real, too. Marissa has work in publications including *RATTLE, StorySouth,* and *Future Cycle.*

Peggy Muir is a Mainer retired from teaching anthropology, American Studies, and women's studies at secondary and university levels. Peggy and her artist husband Bryce wrote about art, the Iles-de-la-Madeleine, Quebec (where Peggy did fieldwork on women's work), maritime culture, and their 29,000 mile US tour (*www.americansabbatical.com*). Her challenges as a widow include solo sailing the sloop Bryce built, and nurturing the local arts center started in his spirit (*www. merrymeetingarts-center.org*). Her greatest joys are her son, daughter-in-law, grandboy, friends, walks, reading, art, gardening, sailing.

Sheryl L. Nelms is from Marysville, Kansas. She graduated from South Dakota State University in Family Relations and Child Development. She has had over 5,000 articles, stories and poems published, including *Bluebonnets, Boots and Buffalo Bones,* from Laughing Cactus Press imprint of Silver Boomer Books and thirteen other individual collections of her poems. She is the fiction/nonfiction editor of *The Pen Woman Magazine*, the National League of American Pen Women publication and a recent Pushcart Prize nominee.

Linda O'Connell is a widely published inspirational writer and poet. Her work appears in several Silver Boomer anthologies, *Chicken Soup for the Soul* books, *Sasse, Reminisce Magazine,* and more. She finds humor in everyday living. Positive thinking helps her get through each day. *lindaoconnell.blogspot.com.*

Karen O'Leary is a wife, mother, nurse, and freelance writer from West Fargo, North Dakota. She has published poetry, short stories, and articles in a variety of venues including *Sketchbook, Poems of the World, The Shine Journal, Haiku Pix, From the Porch Swing,* and *The Journal of Christian Nursing.* In 2011, she released her first book of poetry, *Whispers.* Writing is a blessing in her life.

Helen Padway has poetry in ezines and print publications. Recent print publications include *Verse*

Wisconsin and *Wisconsin Poets' Calendar.* Theater trained, she worked both in television and radio writing and performing. After a hiatus for marriage and children (five), in widowhood she picked up her pen again. She is active in the Wisconsin Poetry community and continues to study to perfect her craft, attending workshops throughout the USA. She is part of The Sparks and the Hartford Avenue Poets. She believes that poets tell the truth, foresee the future and make the world a better place.

Carl Palmer, twice nominated for the Micro Award in flash fiction and thrice for the Pushcart Prize in poetry, is from Old Mill Road in Ridgeway, Virginia. Carl now lives in University Place, Washington. MOTTO: Long Weekends Forever.

Linda A. Panczner hopes to inspire the students she teaches at the University of Toledo that there's more to writing than essays and reports. Free-lance writing reaches into the heart and probes the soul, frees the unexpressed, and gives form to those elusive insights that just have to be pronounced. She has been published in newspapers, magazines, and anthologies.

Carol Faulkner Peck taught at University of Maryland for over thirty years, was Writer/Composer-in-Residence at Sidwell Friends School in Washington, DC, and has conducted Artists-in-Education poetry workshops in schools since 1971. She also works with at-risk teens, hospice patients, and prison inmates. Her publications include *From Deep Within: Poetry Workshops in Nursing Homes,* "I Ain't Gonna Wrote No Pome!", two children's musicals, and several articles and poems in *Christian Science Monitor, Michigan Quarterly Review, Virginia Quarterly Review, South Coast Journal, Little Patuxen Review,* and other journals. She was widowed in September 2011, and is experiencing healing through writing.

"One often calms one's grief by recounting it." Pierre Corneille ~§~

Joan Peronto is a transplanted mid-westerner having graduated from the University of Wisconsin, Madison. She worked as a reference librarian for thirty years and has been published in *Crossing Paths*, an anthology of western New England poets, *The Berkshire Review, The Berkshire Sampler, Hummingbird* and *The Rockford Review*.

Mary Pfeiffer, an author from her teens when she wrote a weekly newspaper column, taught English and now teaches memoir writing at Collin College. She speaks to groups about memoirs, sharing her writings. Her "Persimmon Seeds," was included in *Ten Spurs*, the Mayborn Literary Nonfiction Conference's top ten selections, published by the University of North Texas. She has roots in Missouri where her extended family still lives but calls herself Texan, having lived there long enough to raise two daughters and retire from a teaching career.

Carol McAdoo Rehme's own life was altered witnessing her mother's brave journey through widowhood. An award-winning author and editor, Carol writes prolifically about small moments with large impacts, moments common to us all. She is the co-author of five gift books. Learn about her newly-released biography, *Finding the Pearl,* at *rehme.com*.

Penny Righthand grew up in New York, went to school in Michigan, studied creative writing in Washington State, and settled in Oakland, California. She writes a nonfiction column for the professional journal *Advisor Today*. She has a busy financial advising practice, coaches her three grandsons in various sports, and travels widely. Most of her writing is in hundreds of notebooks and computers in her home. She has been a widow for four years.

Stella Rimmer is 73 years old and has been weaving her way through the web of widowhood for many years. Having always enjoyed writing she has kept a diary since

"Part of every misery is...the misery's shadow or reflection: the fact that

the age of nine, which served as a vehicle in which to express herself and record the various stages of her life. She recently joined a creative nonfiction writing group, inspiring her to write essays on various themes and presently she is working on the story about her late husband's two heart transplants, which she hopes to complete in the not-too-distant future.

Barbara B. Rollins, writer, editor and publisher with Silver Boomer Books, takes advice from her sons when they are right and explores what she chooses — her favorite activity being hugging twin grandsons. Her Eagle Wings Press books *A Time for Verse – Poetic Ponderings on Ecclesiastes* and *A Cloud of Witnesses – Two Big Books and Us,* added to a series of juvenile forensic books and the young adult novel *Syncopated Summer,* make this anthology the fourteenth book bearing her name.

Lessa Roskin and husband Michael raised their three children in Israel. She enjoyed her fruitful career as a speech and language pathologist. After her husband died she began to express her bereavement through poetry. She has organized support groups for widows in the Jerusalem area.

Helen Ruggieri has a new book of poems called *Butterflies Under A Japanese Moon* from Kitsune Press. She had an essay about learning to use the library in *Flashlight Memories.*

Wayne Scheer has been nominated for four Pushcart Prizes and a Best of the Net. He's published stories, poems and essays, in print and online, including *Revealing Moments,* a collection of flash stories, published by Thumbscrews Press. (*issuu.com/pearnoir/docs/revealing_moments*) Wayne lives in Atlanta and can be contacted at wvscheer@aol.com.

you don't merely suffer but have to keep on thinking about the fact

Molly Seale holds an MFA in Theatre from The University of Texas, Austin and has most recently taught in the University Honors Program at Southern Illinois University, Carbondale, teaching Death Onstage and Anatomy of Loss: Death and Dying, Grief and Grieving. She is a passionate writer of plays, poems, fiction and nonfiction.

Marian Kaplun Shapiro is the author of a professional book, *Second Childhood* (Norton, 1988); a poetry book, *Players In The Dream, Dreamers In The Play* (Plain View Press, 2007), and two chapbooks: *Your Third Wish*, (Finishing Line, 2007); and *The End Of The World, Announced On Wednesday* (Pudding House, 2007). She practices as a psychologist, and is a member of the Cambridge Friends Meeting. Having had the good luck to choose a great husband at age twenty, she has been married for 52 years, and is the mother of two and grandmother of five. A resident of Lexington, she is the winner of about forty poetry prizes. She was named Senior Poet Laureate of Massachusetts in 2006, in 2008, in 2010, and 2011.

Aline Soules' work has appeared in journals, ezines, and anthologies such as *100 Words, Literature of the Expanding Frontier,* and *Variations on the Ordinary. The Size of the World* was co-published with *The Shape of the Heart* by Plain View Press. *Meditations on Woman* was published by Anaphora Literary Press in 2011. Poems from her chapbook *Evening Sun: A Widow's Journey* appeared in *Kaleidowhirl, Reed, Shaking Like a Mountain, The Houston Literary Review,* and others. Her blog is at *alinesoules.wordpress. com.*

Julie Stuckey grew up in Pennsylvania, graduated from the University of Delaware with a degree in Business/ Philosophy concentration and currently lives in upstate New York. She is especially drawn to writing that is firmly rooted in the imagery of the natural world and has had numerous

that you suffer." C.S. Lewis ~§~ *"Suppressed grief suffocates, it rages*

poems published online, in print journals and in anthologies. Several of her poems have received Finalist or Honorable Mention in various contests.

Marian Veverka received her BFA in Creative writing at the age of 47. She has written novels, short stories and creative non-fiction. Her most recent poetry has appeared in *Barefoot Review, Curio, Moondance Magazine, Verse Wisconsin, Camel Saloon* and the anthology *Bigger than they Appear.* In 2006 she became a widow after 52 years of marriage. She is the mother of six children and many grandchildren and great grandchildren. She lives in the country and enjoys writing about the natural world.

Phyllis Wax, a Pushcart nominee poet, lives and writes in Milwaukee on a bluff overlooking Lake Michigan. Her poetry has appeared in *Out of Line, Ars Medica, Verse Wisconsin, Your Daily Poem, The New Verse News, Naugatuck River Review, A Prairie Journal,* as well as other journals and anthologies, both print and online. Her work was included in exhibitions of "Threaded Metaphors: Text & Textiles," collaborations between five poets and five fiber artists. Travel, nature and the news provide much of her inspiration. She may be contacted at poetwax@yahoo.com.

Patricia Wellingham-Jones is a former psychology researcher and nurse, also a writer and editor, published widely in journals, anthologies and Internet magazines, including *HazMat Review, Ibbetson Street, Edgz* and *Wicked Alice.* She has a special interest in healing writing and leads a writing group at a cancer center. She writes for the review department of *Recovering the Self: a journal of hope and healing.* Among her ten chapbooks are *Don't Turn Away: poems about breast cancer, End-Cycle: poems about caregiving, Apple Blossoms at Eye Level, Voices on the Land* and *Hormone Stew.*

Jane Willingham, born in 1930, is a pianist, a poet, and a storyteller. Before moving to Maryland in 1997 she taught literature and composition in a Texas community college for 25 years. She is active in her church and in Annapolis Senior Center. She has an Australian Terrier, Lulu, a cat, Lucy, one son in Annapolis, another in Washington state, and four grandchildren.

Laura Madeline Wiseman has a doctorate from the University of Nebraska-Lincoln where she teaches English. She is the author of five chapbooks, including *Branding Girls* (Finishing Line Press, 2011) and *She who Loves Her Father* (Dancing Girl Press, 2012). Her poetry has appeared in *Margie, Feminist Studies, Poet Lore, Cream City Review, The Sow's Ear Poetry Review* and elsewhere. Her prose has appeared in *Arts & Letters, Spittoon, Blackbird, American Short Fiction, 13th Moon,* and elsewhere. Her reviews have appeared in *Prairie Schooner, Valparaiso Poetry Review, 42Opus,* and elsewhere. *www.LauraMadelineWiseman.com.*

Charlotte Wolf sixteen years ago left beautiful Bucks County, Pennsylvania for the even more compelling Blue Ridge Mountains of North Carolina. Several writing classes and critique sessions later, and much to her delight, her short stories and poems have been published in local anthologies, journals, and magazines.

Thelma Zirkelbach was a romance author until her husband's death propelled her from the romance genre to creative nonfiction and poetry. She is a speech-language pathologist in private practice, working with young children who have speech, language and reading disabilities. A voracious reader, she belongs to two book clubs, enjoys cooking, traveling and spending time with her granddaughter. She lives in Houston with two cats to keep her company.

Editing Grief

The Ensemble

writers on four continents
editors in four cities
new friends, faces unknown
voices ringing out across the internet.
synapses of brains, of computers

electronic shuffling of precious life-bits
like robots sorting through grandma's attic
nameless, faceless "editors" making judgments
on which wounded hearts
are strong enough to stand in a line-up
true enough to speak for a group
whose members suffer uniquely alone

past, future, present
strength, hope, cope, aching, longing

"And they shall be one flesh"
let no one put asunder
but it happens and one whole
becomes half

Oh my...oh no...too, too...
something isn't right...seriously?
alone lonely solitary sole
individual unique rare special peerless
a commencement, not an epilogue

Attributions

The following selections included in *On Our Own – Widowhood for Smarties* were previously published as noted below. The authors retain all copyright to the work.

"After Your Husband Dies," *New Purlieu Review*, July 2012 ~§~ "The Aging Widow Understands," *Sugar Mule* ~§~ "All His Heroes," *quint*, journal of University College of the North, Canada ~§~ "Apart," *The Houston Literary Review*, May 2009; and *Qarrtsiluni*, August 20, 2010, nominated for a Pushcart Prize ~§~ "Bouncing Back," expanded version of a blog post at *Widowsphere.blogspot.com* ~§~ "Comforter," limited edition chapbook, *Mothersongs*, by Becky McClure Haigler, 1996 ~§~ "Creeping through Horseradish," *Widowsphere.blogspot.com* ~§~ "End and Beginning" won the New Hampshire Poetry Society contest in 2011 and was featured in their journal, *The Poet's Touchstone*. ~§~ "First Anniversary," *Lunarosity*, 2009 ~§~ "First Christmas Again," *Voices on the Land*, 2004; and *LongStory Short*, 2006 ~§~ "The First Night," *Survivor Chronicles*, May 29, 2010, thesurvivorchronicles.org ~§~ "From Bride to Widow," *AuthorsDen.com*, *BookRix.com*, *The American Widow Project*, and on the author's personal blog, *Memoirs From Nam* ~§~ "Gone? Not Really," chapbook 2008, by Gail Denham ~§~ "Hell, I Forgot Red!" *Knock* at Antioch University of Seattle ~§~ "Her Candle," *Poetic Hours*, issue #24, Spring 2005 ~§~ "The Huntress," *Family Matters* ~§~ "It's a Date," *Every Mom's Soul*, 2005 ~§~ "Little Knives," "Night," and "No Mind a Whetstone," *In the Shadow of the Shoah*, selected poems by Frieda W. Landau, Poetica Publishing 2011 ~§~ "Morning, Third Sunday in June" and "Keep Watering," *Free Verse* (now *Verse Wisconsin*) May/June 2003 ~§~ "New Perspective," *Sandcutters*, Volume 42, Issue 4, 2008, from the Arizona State Poetry Society ~§~ "Pruning Time," *Lubbock Magazine*, 1998 ~§~ "The Room Where You Died," *End-Cycle: Poems about caregiving*, 2007; and *Chiron Review*, 2009 ~§~ "Sleeping Alone," *Poetry Hickory*, 2011 ~§~ "Soaked into that Room," *Rattlesnake Review*, 2008 ~§~ "Stepping Out," *Sentinel Literary Magazine*, August 2010 ~§~ "There's No One," *From My Heart*, by Lessa Roskin ~§~ "Winter Damage," *Mulled Words – a Winter Anthology*

Other books from

Silver Boomer Books:

Anthologies

Silver Boomers
prose and poetry by and about baby boomers

Freckles to Wrinkles

This Path

From the Porch Swing
memories of our grandparents

Flashlight Memories

The Harsh and the Heart
Celebrating the Military

A Quilt of Holidays
Stories, Poetry, Memoir

Single Author Books

Song of County Roads
by Ginny Greene

Crazy Lady in the Mirror
by Madelyn Kamen

Books from Eagle Wings Press
imprint of Silver Boomer Books

Slender Steps to Sanity
Twelve-Step Notes of Hope
by OAStepper, Compulsive Overeater

Writing Toward the Light
A Grief Journey
by Laura Flett

A Time for Verse
poetic ponderings on Ecclesiastes
by Barbara B. Rollins

Survived to Love
by Edward L. Hennessy (Ed H)

White Elephants
by Chynna T. Laird

A Cloud of Witnesses
Two Big Books and Us
by Barbara B. Rollins with OAStepper

Insights from the Jobsite
by Robyn Conley

Books from Laughing Cactus Press
imprint of Silver Boomer Books

Poetry Floats
New and selected Philosophy-lite
by Jim Wilson

Bluebonnets, Boots and Buffalo Bones
by Sheryl L. Nelms

not so GRIMM
gentle fables and cautionary tales
by Becky Haigler

Three Thousand Doors
by Karen Elaine Greene

Milagros
by Tess Almendárez Lojacono

CPSIA information can be obtained at www.ICGtesting.com
Printed in the USA
LVOW120931080912

297954LV00002B/2/P